Euripides: Medea

Euripides
Medea

A new translation and
commentary by John Harrison

Introduction to the Greek Theatre
by P.E. Easterling

Series Editors: John Harrison and Judith Affleck

CAMBRIDGE UNIVERSITY PRESS
Cambridge, New York, Melbourne, Madrid, Cape Town, Singapore, São Paulo

Cambridge University Press
The Edinburgh Building, Cambridge CB2 2RU, UK

www.cambridge.org
Information on this title: www.cambridge.org/9780521644792

First published 2000
7th printing 2005

Printed in the United Kingdom at the University Press, Cambridge

A catalogue record for this publication is available from the British Library

ISBN-13 978-0-521-64479-2 paperback
ISBN-10 0-521-64479-8 paperback

PERFORMANCE
For permission to give a public performance of *Medea* please
write to Permissions Department, Cambridge University Press,
The Edinburgh Building, Shaftesbury Road, Cambridge CB2 2RU.

ACKNOWLEDGEMENTS
Thanks are due to the following for permission to reproduce pictures:

p. 32, 40, 105 © Ivan Kyncl; p. 66 © John Haynes; p. 82 Staatliche
Antikensammlung und Glyptothek München. Photo: Christa Koppermann;
p. 90 © The Cleveland Museum of Art, 1999, Leonard C. Hanna Jr. Fund,
1999.1; p. 108, Fig. A from p. 151 of *The Cambridge Ancient History, Plates to
Volumes V and VI*, © Cambridge University Press.

Map on p. 110 by Helen Humphries.

Cover picture: Medea, by Bernard Safran, reproduced by kind permission of the
Estate of Bernard Safran.

Contents

Preface

The aim of the series is to enable students to approach Classical plays with confidence and understanding: to discover the play within the text.

The translations are new. Many recent versions of Greek tragedy have been done by poets and playwrights who do not work from the original Greek. The translators of this series aim to bring readers, actors and directors as close as possible to the playwrights' actual words and intentions: to create translations which are faithful to the original in content and tone; and which are speakable, with the immediacy of modern English.

The notes are designed for students of Classical Civilisation and Drama, and indeed anyone who is interested in theatre. They address points which present difficulty to the reader of today: chiefly relating to the Greeks' religious and moral attitudes, their social and political life, and mythology.

Our hope is that students should explore the play for themselves. The conventions of the Classical theatre are discussed, but there is no thought of recommending 'authentic' performances. Different groups will find different ways of responding to each play. The best way of bringing alive an ancient play, as any other, is to explore the text practically, to stimulate thought about ways of staging the plays today. Stage directions in the text are minimal, and the notes are not prescriptive; rather, they contain questions and exercises which explore the dramatic qualities of the text. Bullet points introduce suggestions for discussion and analysis; open bullet points focus on more practical exercises.

If the series encourages students to attempt a staged production, so much the better. But the primary aim is understanding and enjoyment.

The translation of *Medea* is based on the Greek text, edited by J. Diggle for Oxford University Press. Numbers in square brackets at the bottom of each page of translation refer to the lines of the Greek text; line references in the notes and elsewhere refer to this translation.

John Harrison
Judith Affleck

Background to the story of Medea

This story is told in a variety of ways, most famously by Apollonius of Rhodes in his romantic epic *The Voyage of the Argo* which was written in the 3rd century BC.

Medea was the granddaughter of the Sun. Her father was Aeëtes who was King of Colchis, at the eastern end of the Black Sea. In his kingdom was the Golden Fleece, a treasure that was guarded by a dragon. Medea met Jason when he came to Colchis in quest of the Golden Fleece.

Jason was the rightful king of the Greek state of Iolcus (modern Volos). While he was too young to rule he went away to be educated by the centaur Chiron, and his uncle Pelias reigned in his place. When Jason was old enough to return to Iolcus, Pelias was reluctant to give up the throne. He asked Jason what one should do to rid oneself of a man by whom one felt threatened. 'Send him to get the Golden Fleece,' said Jason. Pelias took the advice and Jason accepted the challenge.

Jason assembled an expedition of fifty of the noblest heroes. They sailed in the ship *Argo*, the first long ship, built with pines cut from the peninsula of Pelion near Iolcus. The expedition sailed through the straits of Bosporus, which were flanked by the formidable Clashing Rocks, and into the Black Sea. After many adventures they came to Colchis. Aeëtes was reluctant to part with the Fleece, but offered it to Jason if he could perform a series of difficult tasks. Jason had first to yoke two monstrous, fire-breathing bulls and plough with them; sow some dragon's teeth, from which would spring armed warriors whom he had to kill; then overcome the dragon which guarded the Fleece. Aeëtes was confident that the tasks were too difficult for Jason. But he did not reckon with Jason's divine protector, Hera, the Queen of the gods, who persuaded Aphrodite, the goddess of love, to make Medea fall in love with Jason. With the help of Medea's magic powers, he accomplished all the tasks.

Having betrayed her father, Medea was forced to flee with Jason back to his native Greece. In some way, during the flight, Medea's brother Apsyrtus was murdered. In one version of the story his dismembered body was scattered at sea, to delay the pursuing Aeëtes, who would be obliged to collect the pieces. In Euripides' play, Medea is said by Jason to have killed her brother at the family hearth.

After many adventures the *Argo* returned to Iolcus where Pelias was still king. Medea again used her magic skills, offering to show Pelias' daughters how to rejuvenate their ageing father. She cut a ram into pieces and boiled these in a cauldron with magic herbs; the ram emerged as a newborn lamb. But when the daughters cut up and boiled Pelias, Medea withheld the crucial herbs. She and Jason were forced to flee again and came as refugees to Corinth, where this play takes place.

List of characters

NURSE

MEDEA AND JASON'S TWO SONS

THE BOYS' TUTOR

MEDEA

JASON

CREON   *King of Corinth*

AEGEUS   *King of Athens*

MESSENGER

CHORUS OF CORINTHIAN WOMEN

PROLOGUE (LINES 1–120)

Some Greek plays began with a dialogue between two characters. Euripides preferred to have a single character introduce himself or herself and the dramatic situation.

1, 2 Argo, Colchis: (See Background to the story (page v) and map (page 111).) Throughout the play there are references to sailing. The play's first audience (at Athens in 431 BC), like the play's characters, were familiar with sea travel.

In legend *Argo* was the first ship. Some writers, believing that sailing was a violation of nature, traced back human suffering to this original sin.

7 smitten with love: The Greek phrase suggests that this is no ordinary love. Extreme sexual passion, in ancient as in modern drama, can prove dangerous. See Medea (line 319) and the Chorus (414, 619–23).

9 Corinth: This was a busy mercantile city whose citizens would be accustomed to foreigners in their midst.

11 The people here are well disposed: It was a deep-seated principle for the Greeks to offer welcome and hospitality to strangers. (For example, in *Odyssey vi–viii* the Phaeacians' welcome to the shipwrecked stranger Odysseus.)

17 the princess: She has no name here, though in some versions of the story she is called Glauce.

Vows and promises

19 her loss of honour: Medea feels dishonoured and wronged (25, 32), but she cannot stop Jason.

When Medea fled from Colchis she did not have a conventional contract of marriage that had been negotiated between her father and Jason with an agreed dowry. Even if she had such a contract, a wife was effectively the husband's possession and he could divorce her at will. (See note on page 14.) All Medea has to rely on are Jason's '**great oaths**' (20, 152).

Oaths had a special sanctity in the ancient world because they were protected by Zeus. Medea is looking not simply for sympathy as a wife abandoned in a foreign city. Jason has neglected his debt to her for all the services she has given to him (22). He has also broken the oaths which he swore to her. So Medea claims the support of the gods, whose divinity Jason has abused (21).

28 Like a stone or wave:
● What ideas do these similes suggest?

MEDEA

NURSE If only the *Argo* had never winged its way
   To Colchis, through the blue-grey Clashing Rocks!
   If the pines on Pelion's glens had never fallen
   To the axe, and those heroes never pulled the oars,
   Who went, at Pelias' bidding, to find the Golden Fleece!   5
   Then my mistress Medea would not have sailed
   To the towers of Iolcus, her heart smitten with love
   For Jason. Nor would she have induced Pelias' daughters
   To kill their father, nor come here to live in Corinth
   With her husband and their children.   10
   The people here are well disposed to her,
   An exile and Jason's all-obedient wife:
   That's the best way for a woman to keep safe –
   Not to cross her husband.
   But now her deepest love is sick; all turns to hate.   15
   Jason has betrayed his own sons and my mistress –
   Left her for a royal wedding-bed. He's married the princess,
   The daughter of King Creon.
   Poor Medea rages at her loss of honour,
   Cries out he swore an oath, recalls the powerful pledge   20
   He made to her, and calls the gods to witness
   How Jason thanks her for her loyalty.
   She does not eat. She gives herself to grief,
   Wasting away her time in tears.
   Ever since she knew her husband's wrong to her,   25
   She's lain, her eyes fixed on the ground.
   When friends reason with her, she listens
   Like a stone or wave of the sea;
   Just, sometimes, turning that pale neck of hers
   She wails aloud for her dear father,   30
   Her country and her home, which she betrayed

36 dreadful plan: The reference to Medea's hatred of her sons is dramatically placed, just before their entry.
- Do you think the Nurse has a clear idea what the plan is?

The Nurse's speech
The Nurse expresses both anxiety and a longing to undo the past.
- Why do you think Euripides gave the introductory speech to a servant? Are there advantages in her being an old servant of Medea?
- What impression do you get of the character of the Nurse?
- Explore the changes of subject matter in the speech. Is there a predominant mood?
- Speak the whole speech, first as if speaking thoughts aloud, then as if addressing the audience. Which is the more effective?

39 here come the boys: There are no stage directions in the original text. Entrances are usually signalled by characters on stage. (Exits are often not indicated.)

The boys are young, but old enough presumably to understand what others say to them. For most of the play they do not speak, but they are a focus of attention and sympathy throughout.

Child actors are not always available.
- If there are no children to play the parts in a production, can you think of another suitable way of representing them? (For example, in a celebrated production in Berlin the two children were represented by white statues, 'to allow the audience to move beyond horror at the infanticide and engage more directly with the psychological complexity behind it'.)

Entreaties
57 Please: The Greek means literally 'by your chin'.
The Nurse, in pleading with the Tutor to tell her what he has heard, touches his chin. When an entreaty or supplication is reinforced by such a ritual gesture, the person to whom the appeal is made feels under pressure to grant the request. The suppliant may clasp the other's knees or grasp his right hand or touch his chin. This custom will prove important in this play.

When she came here with the man who now dishonours her.
Poor woman, she's learnt from misfortune what it is
To lose one's fatherland.
She hates her sons, takes no pleasure in seeing them. 35
I'm afraid she's dreaming up some dreadful plan.
She is dangerous. None who makes an enemy of her
Will win an easy victory.
But here come the boys, back from their game.
They have no idea of their mother's troubles. 40
Young minds are still untouched by grief.

TUTOR Old servant of my mistress' home,
Why are you standing all alone here by the door,
Bewailing your troubles to yourself?
How does Medea like being left alone by you? 45

NURSE Old man, tutor of Jason's sons,
Good servants share their masters' sufferings –
They touch our hearts. I find it so distressing,
I had to come out here to tell my mistress' woes
To the earth and sky. 50

TUTOR Poor woman! Has she not yet stopped her crying?

NURSE Stopped! Her misery has just begun: it's not yet reached half-way.

TUTOR Poor fool! – if I may call my mistress that –
She knows nothing of the latest troubles.

NURSE What's happened? Tell me, don't hold it back. 55

TUTOR Nothing. I regret saying what I did.

NURSE Please, don't keep a secret from a fellow slave:
I will keep quiet, if I must.

TUTOR I was walking past the seats, where the old men
Play dice, by the sacred fountain of Peirene. 60
I pretended not to listen,
But heard one say that King Creon intends
To send the boys away with their mother,
Expel them from the country. Whether the story's true
I don't know, but I wouldn't want it so. 65

The importance of sons

The Nurse (66) expresses surprise that Jason feels indifference about his sons. A father, as head of his household (*oikos* or *domos*), was owed total obedience by his sons. He could renounce or disinherit them, but he expected them to look after him in old age and to defend his honour and reputation after death (for example, Orestes was obliged to avenge his dead father, Agamemnon). It was a matter of honour that the *oikos* should not die out or be destroyed, and it was through his sons that a man perpetuated his *oikos*.

The Nurse and the Tutor

Both these long-standing servants of the family are slaves. Slaves commonly appear in the plays of all the Greek tragedians, but they were thought to be a particular feature of Euripides' work. The character Euripides in Aristophanes' comedy *Frogs* is proud that in his plays a cross-section of society had a voice: 'women and slaves, master, virgin, old crone, all talked … that was democratic'. In fact, in the Athenian democracy women and slaves took no part.

- Which of the words of the Nurse and the Tutor enable us to establish their attitudes and relationship?
- Explore ways of presenting these two characters and their meeting, remembering the presence of the children.

83 like a wild bull: It is common in epic poetry for heroes to be compared to powerful animals.

- How does this comparison affect our view of Medea?

Friends and enemies (86)

In the ancient world it was believed that it was a matter of pride, duty (and pleasure) to harm one's enemies (*echthroi*). For example in Sophocles' *Ajax*, the hero, feeling his honour slighted, wishes on his enemies the vilest of deaths. Conversely, it was one's duty to help friends and dear ones (*philoi*, 'dear ones', embraces all who are close, such as members of the family and friends).

Medea feels that her honour has been slighted. Jason, by betraying her, is no longer a *philos* but an *echthros* (69).

Music

Medea's first cry, from inside the house, introduces a lyric section (one accompanied by music) which continues until her entrance onto the stage. The iambic metre, used for spoken dialogue, gives way to musical rhythms. The words would have been sung or chanted and accompanied at times by pipes and tympani. (See note on page 12.) Lyric sections are centred in the text.

NURSE What, will Jason let his sons be treated
       Like that, even if he's quarrelled with their mother?
TUTOR His new marriage now comes first.
       He is no friend to this house.
NURSE We're lost, then, if we must face new miseries,   70
       Before we've drained our present cup.
TUTOR But keep quiet. Say nothing. This isn't the moment
       For Medea to learn this.
NURSE Children, do you hear what sort of father Jason is
       To you? Curse him! – no, he is my master –   75
       But he's proved himself a traitor to his family.
TUTOR He's no worse than others. Are you just finding out
       That people love themselves more than their neighbour?
       With his new lover, Jason has no time for the boys.
NURSE Go into the house, boys. It will be all right.   80
       (*to Tutor*) Keep them as much as possible on their own,
       Don't let them near Medea in her present mood.
       I've seen her eyeing them, like a wild bull,
       As if there's something that she means to do.
       She'll not give up her anger till she has struck –   85
       Let's hope it is her enemies, not these dear ones!

MEDEA   (*off stage*) Oh misery! How wretched I am!
                     I want to die!
NURSE   There it is, my darlings! Your mother
                 Racks her feelings, fans her rage.   90
                     Quick, hurry in,
                   Don't let her see you.
                  Keep well away, take care.
                 She can be wild and hateful,
                     In her stubborn pride.   95
           Go on, as fast as you can, indoors.

98 It is a cloud she will ignite:
● What does this striking metaphor suggest about the Nurse's fears?

110 Beware a royal temper:
● The Nurse's views (110–17) would appeal to the Athenian audience, whose democratic constitution was based on the principle of equality – among male citizens (for the position of women, see note on 220).Who is the Nurse thinking of (110)? Is it clear? (See note on 798.)

Excess

118 Excess brings no benefit: It was commonly accepted in Greek thought, that moderation is wise and safe. Going beyond what is one's natural and rightful lot incurs the anger of the gods.

The Nurse's words (100, 161, 173), and Medea's first lines off stage, suggest anything but moderation in Medea's behaviour – she is on a different scale from ordinary people and is therefore dangerous.

PARODOS (ENTRY OF THE CHORUS) (121–202)

The Chorus (women of Corinth) are drawn to the scene. This entry is unlike the usual, more formal, entries of many plays in which the Chorus come on singing a structured ode. In *Medea* they enter during a lyrical passage, and their first urgent, short lines are easily integrated in the mood of agitation created by Medea's cries.

At the time of *Medea*'s first production (431 BC) there were fifteen members in the Chorus. They entered from the sides (*parodoi*) and performed in the open space of the *orchēstra*. Viewed from above by the audience in the tiered seating, their dance and patterns of choreographed movement were an important element in the expressiveness of Greek theatre. (See Introduction to the Greek Theatre, page 107.)

On the modern stage it is common to have fewer chorus members.
○ What would be the relevant considerations in deciding how many chorus members to have? Would it be adequate to have only one?

The Greek 'family'

127 The family is finished: The Greeks did not have a word equivalent to our 'family'. Their words for 'house' (*oikos* 119, *domos* 105 and 127, *dōma* 125) described an institution more like our 'household', presided over by the male master (*kurios*) who in this case is Jason. These words are sometimes translated as 'house', sometimes as 'family'.

I hear the first danger sign,

Her wailing. It is a cloud she will ignite

To flame as her fury grows.

What will she do, that great, passionate soul,   100

Implacable, stung by misfortune?

MEDEA Aiai. Wronged. My wrongs call forth great cries of woe!

Boys, your mother's hated. Cursed boys,

I wish you dead, your father too.

Curse his whole house!   105

NURSE Oh dear! The children! What have they to do

With their father's wickedness?

Why hate them? Children, I'm sick with worry

That you will come to harm.

Beware a royal temper. Those who have power   110

Aren't used to taking orders;

It's hard to make them change their mood.

Better to live on equal terms

With others. I'd feel safest growing old

In modest ways.   115

The middle course is best in name

And practice, the best policy by far.

Excess brings no benefit to us,

Only greater disasters on a house,

When God is angry.   120

CHORUS I heard her voice, I heard that unhappy woman

From Colchis crying. Still she is not quiet.

Tell us, Nurse. At the gate I heard her

Crying inside the house.

I don't like to see the family suffering.   125

I sympathise with them.

NURSE The family is finished, it's all over here.

Jason's home is now the princess' bed,

Medea is in her room, wasting away,

Letting no friend comfort her   130

With cheering words.

Medea's first words

Medea speaks off stage four times, each time at slightly greater length (87–8, 102–5, 132–6, 149–57).

Analyse her words carefully.

- What are her predominant feelings?
- What do we learn of her desire for revenge?
- Do her words confirm, or differ from, the Nurse's fears?

Gods

Often a god had more than one role or function, and prayers were directed to the appropriate deity or group of deities.

Zeus (137) was the supreme god of the Greeks with a wide range of concerns. He was associated with justice; protector of law and morals; guardian of suppliants, strangers and beggars; and (this is important, as we have already seen) god of oaths. He was also god of the household.

Earth (Ge or Gaia) **and Light** (the Sun) (137) are more elemental deities. There are several significant appeals to the Sun/Helios (from whom Medea traced descent – see Background to the story) and Earth in the play. (See note on page 66.)

Themis (149) was originally identified with Gaia (Earth), and came to stand for 'right' or 'justice'.

Artemis (149) was a daughter of Zeus. She was a huntress and was associated with the wild nature of forests and hills. She herself was a virgin; but, as a god, she was a bringer of fertility and helper of women in childbirth.

- Why do you think the Chorus and Medea call upon these particular five gods?

141 that bed: The Chorus mean 'death'.
Notice how they emphasise the sexual side of Medea's loss in this speech.

156 my country, which I lost: In her distress Medea's thoughts turn to her home and fatherland, but the place which would be her natural refuge is barred to her.
See Index, Medea – thoughts of home.

MEDEA	Aiai.
	Lightning, pierce my head!
	What point is there in living?
	Oh, oh, I want to end my hateful life,
	Leave it behind and die.
CHORUS	Zeus and Earth and Light!
	You hear the poor young wife
	Sing her cry of woe?
	You're mad. What is this longing
	For that bed which none should crave?
	Death's ending will be on you:
	Do not pray for that.
	If your husband adores his new love,
	Let that be: do not vex yourself.
	Leave it to Zeus to see justice done.
	Do not waste away like this,
	Mourning the partner of your bed.
MEDEA	Mighty Themis! Queen Artemis!
	Do you see how I am treated,
	Though I bound my cursed husband
	By great oaths?
	I long to see him and his new bride
	Crushed to pieces, and the whole palace,
	For the wrong they dare to do to me.
	O my father and my country, which I lost,
	When I foully murdered my brother!
NURSE	You hear what she says, calling on
	Themis, who hears our prayers,
	And Zeus, the guardian of mortals' oaths?
	Only some momentous act
	Can stop my mistress' rage.
CHORUS	If only she would come out
	And we could speak to her face to face.
	If only she would drop her present mood,
	Her anger and resentment.
	Let me never fail
	To help my friends.

135

140

145

150

155

160

165

170 We are her friends: The Chorus are well disposed to Medea (126, 168, see also 11). The 'friends' whose sympathy she has rejected (27, 130) may be among the Chorus women.

● How does the Chorus' reaction differ from that of the Nurse?

179 A lioness: Here is a second, powerful animal simile, again suggesting savage power, but here also protective maternal feelings.

In Homer's *Iliad xvii*, the hero Ajax protects the corpse of his ally Patroclus 'like a lion, confronted by huntsmen as he leads his cubs through the forest, plants himself in front of the helpless creatures, breathing defiance and lowering his brows to veil his eyes'.

The character of the Nurse

The Nurse is slow to go and fetch Medea. She wishes that the power of music were exploited as a therapy in curing grief rather than in entertaining people at feasts and banquets. It is hard to know how much music was used for personal solace, but certainly it was a regular feature of social events.

● How helpful is the Nurse's speech (174–94) in establishing her character?

202 gate of Pontus: This is the Bosporus, gateway to the Black Sea. The reference reminds us how far Medea is from home (see map on page 111).

Staging the lyric section (87–202)

Lyrical passages, which include the formal choral odes, were an integral feature of Classical Greek theatre. They gave an almost operatic quality to parts of the plays, as well as providing their distinctive structure. Their effect would be to raise the intensity of the words and emotions expressed.

In this passage Medea would have been off stage, the Nurse on stage and the Chorus would be in the *orchēstra*, moving as well as singing.

Even if not sung, words spoken over music can gain impact, and percussion can point up meaning and add emphasis. Even without instruments it is possible, with imagination and care, to create a musical texture.

○ Experiment with patterns of speech, music and movement to develop ideas about how to stage this passage effectively.

○ What would be lost by removing the musical element of the lyrical sections?

We do not see Medea, but we do see the effect of her cries on the Nurse and the Chorus.

○ Explore ways of expressing their agitation and concern, while keeping Medea's words as the main focus of interest.

(*to Nurse*) Go and bring her out. Tell her
We are her friends.   170
Be quick, before she does some harm
To those inside. This grief of hers
Is a mighty force.

NURSE   I will. I am afraid
I'll not persuade the mistress.   175
But I'll gladly try.
And yet when any of the servants comes near her
Or tries to speak, she throws a savage glare
Like a lioness with her cubs.
You could say that men have got things wrong,   180
They've not been very clever:
They've written songs for festivals and feasts
And dinner time – life's sweet music.
But no one has found a way
Of banishing by music and melodious song   185
Men's hellish griefs,
From which spring death and calamities
To ruin families.
There'd be some point in using song
To cure men's suffering.   190
But at a sumptuous feast
Why raise your voice for nothing?
A full meal in itself
Gives pleasure enough.

CHORUS   I heard a wail, full of grievous moans,   195
Shouts of shrill pain and distress,
Against the traitor who has betrayed her bed.
She calls as witness to the wrong she's suffered
Themis, daughter of Zeus, goddess of oaths,
Who guided her across the sea to Greece   200
Through the night waves to the watery strait,
The barrier gate of Pontus.

FIRST EPISODE (203–398)

The character who has been the focus of most of the play so far now appears, possibly accompanied by the Nurse. In Sophocles' *Ajax* and *Philoctetes* the main character is similarly heard off stage before appearing in person.

- What dramatic effect is created here by the delay?
- From her own words uttered off stage, and those of the Nurse and Chorus, what would you expect Medea's mood and behaviour to be? Do her opening words suggest the same mood?

203 I have left the house: Women were, on the whole, expected to remain in the home. The Nurse explained to the Tutor why she was out of doors (43–50).

- What does Medea's justification for coming out tell us about her?

The position of women

220 We women: Medea's words reflect the general position of women in Euripides' time more than her own situation. She voices the grievances of women in a male-dominated society.

The position of women was a subject of contemporary discussion, and there was no more public place in which to air such a topic than before the large audience of citizens in the theatre of Dionysus in Athens. Aristophanes' plays *Lysistrata* and *Ecclesiazusae* portray women in a comic context in revolt against the restrictions placed on them. But Medea's words present an altogether more serious and powerful case. To suggest that childbirth could be more daunting than fighting (239–40) is a startling challenge to the traditional values of the time. Not only was this written by a man and performed by male actors; though our evidence is inconclusive, it is also possible that women (who could not vote, stand for office or even speak in the law courts) were not admitted to the theatre.

Divorce

A woman was typically always under the authority of a male. Before marriage, her male authority (*kurios*) was her father or next of kin. Once married, her *kurios* was her husband. A man could divorce his wife by returning her and her dowry to her father, who could then give her in marriage to another, but, as Medea implies (226), not without some sense of disgrace. The legality of Medea's marriage to Jason is not questioned. She and the Nurse refer always to Jason as Medea's husband (*posis*). But, now she is rejected by her husband, Medea does not have even the refuge of her former home, and therefore she has no legal representation.

MEDEA Women of Corinth, I have left the house, because I don't want
You to blame me. I know that many people can be arrogant
In public and in private. But some are called indifferent   205
To others, just because they are reserved.
There is no justice in the judgements that men make:
Before they know a man's inner self,
They hate at sight, though they've not been wronged.
A foreigner must take special care to conform to the state –   210
Even a citizen who is fool enough
To let his stubborn pride offend his fellow-citizens
Wins no praise from me.
This unexpected blow has broken my heart.
I'm finished. I've lost all joy in life.   215
I want to die, my friends.
The man who was my whole life – I know it well –
My husband, has turned out the most despicable of men.
Of all the creatures that have life and reason
We women have the worst lot.   220
First we have to buy a husband, at vast expense,
And – to make the bargain the more painful –
What we buy is someone to lord it
Over our body. For us, the biggest question is
Whether the man we get is good or bad.   225
Divorce is not respectable for women,
And we may not refuse our husband.
A woman, coming to new ways and laws,
Needs to be clairvoyant – she can't find out at home,
What sort of man will share her bed.   230
If we work at it, and our husband is content
Beneath the marriage yoke,
Life can be enviable. If not, better to be dead.
When a man is tired of the company at home,
He can go out and end his discontent. We women   235
Must have eyes only for one man.

244 stateless: Medea calls herself not only foreign, but 'stateless'. To the Greeks, for whom the state (*polis*) was a necessary condition of civilised life, this was a dreadful fate. In Sophocles' play *Philoctetes*, the hero calls it 'living death'.

245 Plundered: Notice Medea's emotive language, and the risky mention of her brother whom she had helped to kill!

250 say nothing: In Greek plays, the Chorus did not leave the *orchēstra* between their entry and their final exit. So, since here Medea wishes to conceal her plans, they have to be sworn to secrecy. Euripides can from now on give the audience insights into Medea's mind through her confidences to the Chorus.

First impressions of Medea

Medea is a woman, an abandoned wife, a mother, a foreigner, unable to return to her homeland, talking to a group of women whom she may not know well, but who are well disposed to her (170).

- How much importance does she give to being a foreigner? (Do the Chorus treat her as a foreigner?)
- Would any of these adjectives describe Medea: distraught, desperate, controlled, dignified, suicidal, frightening, emotional, calm, manipulative, vulnerable, self-pitying, meek, defiant, cunning? Can you think of others?

The Chorus' response

255 I will: This is the first example of Medea's persuasiveness. Despite 'murderous' (254), the Chorus know no more than we whether Medea has a clear plan of action. They promise to be silent without knowing what Medea intends to do, and accept without question that Medea is justified in seeking revenge (255).

- Contrast this with their response to Medea's earlier cries (144–8).
- Should Medea stand still or approach the women?
- Explore the reaction of the women to her entry, and to her words.

259 Medea, scowling there: Since masks would have been worn in the original production (see Introduction to the Greek Theatre, page 107), it is interesting to speculate whether Medea's fierce look (also 83, 178) would have been incorporated in the mask she wore.

Creon's entry

Creon is probably accompanied by attendants (see 324).

- What is the tone of his first speech? Does it suggest confidence or some insecurity?

They say our life at home is free
From danger, while they go off to war.
The fools! I would rather fight three times
In war, than go through childbirth once! 240
But your case and mine are not the same.
You have your city here, your family home,
Life's pleasures and the company of those dear to you.
I am alone and stateless, dishonoured by my husband:
Plundered from a barbarian land, 245
I have no mother, brother, nor any of my kin,
No haven from this calamity.
And so I ask one thing of you. If I can find a way,
A means of taking my revenge on my husband
For his wrongs, say nothing. 250
A woman is often full of fear, especially when
She's faced with violence and weapons.
But when she's wronged in marriage,
There is no more murderous spirit.

CHORUS I will. You are right to take revenge on your husband. 255
I am not surprised that what has happened grieves you.
But I see Creon, lord of this land, coming here
With some new resolution to announce.

CREON Medea, scowling there with fury at your husband!
I have given orders that you should leave the country: 260
Take your two sons and go, into exile. No delay!
This is my word, I am the judge.
I shall not go back into the palace
Until I've cast you out, beyond our boundaries.

266 full sail: Sometimes, as here, Medea uses metaphors from sea travel (also 745–8 and Chorus, 349). At other times, such as when she says (247) that she has no haven, the nautical phrase is literally true.

270 You frighten me: Creon fears the rage of the scorned woman against his daughter. This fear is the greater when that woman is 'clever' and has Medea's extraordinary skills.

280 my reputation: This must refer to her part in helping Jason to win the Golden Fleece and in Pelias' death. But the Greek word for 'clever' had other connotations for the play's first audience.

'Cleverness'

Medea has to work fast, in response to Creon's announcement.
- What evidence does her behaviour with Creon offer of her cleverness?
- Does it suggest that she knows, and is playing on, his weakness?

Euripides lived in an age of exceptional artistic and intellectual activity. There was a spirit of enquiry and scepticism which alarmed conventional people. The root of the Greek word for 'clever' (*sophos*) is also in the name of the Sophists, teachers who were seen to question traditional values.

Increasingly the Sophists were held responsible for Athens' moral decline and for the eventual defeat of Athens in the Peloponnesian War. The popular suspicion of thinkers and teachers is expressed in Aristophanes' *Clouds*, in which Socrates presides over an academy which claims to be able to teach pupils to make the weaker case in a debate seem the stronger. Euripides too was satirised for his 'advanced' views and his 'modern' style of writing. After the war Socrates was put to death for 'corrupting' the minds of the young; Euripides had already gone to live abroad.
- To what extent do you think Medea's words (280–91) express the feelings of educated women in a male-dominated society?

294–5 Have no fear of me, Creon: Medea has discussed her weakness as a woman and a foreigner. Here she professes her weakness in relation to the ruler of Corinth (see also 301–2). Note that Medea uses Creon's name (it means 'ruler') when she acknowledges his power (see also 269, 325).

MEDEA Aiai. Wretched me! I am utterly destroyed.　265
　　My enemies are in full sail; there is
　　No easy escape from this disaster.
　　But, despite my ill-treatment, I'll speak out:
　　For what offence, Creon, do you banish me?
CREON You frighten me – no point in cloaking what I mean.　270
　　I fear you'll do some irreparable harm
　　To my daughter. I am afraid for many reasons.
　　You are clever, skilled in many evil arts.
　　You resent being deprived of Jason's bed.
　　I hear reports that you are threatening　275
　　Violence on me and on the bridegroom and his bride.
　　I'll make sure that doesn't happen.
　　Better make you my enemy now, madam,
　　Than weaken and regret it.
MEDEA Oh dear! This is not the first time, my reputation　280
　　Has often hurt me, Creon, done me so much harm.
　　No sensible man should have his children
　　Taught to be too clever.
　　They are called idlers, and excite
　　Resentful envy in their fellow citizens.　285
　　Present some clever, new idea to fools –
　　They'll think it's you who are useless and a fool.
　　As for those who think they have a subtle intellect,
　　If you are thought superior in the state, they take it hard.
　　That has been my fate. Because I'm clever,　290
　　Some are jealous, to others I'm objectionable.
　　But I'm not really so clever.
　　You say you are afraid – that I'll do something unpleasant?
　　I'm in no position – have no fear of me, Creon, –
　　To go against those who rule.　295
　　What wrong have you done me?

297 You gave your daughter: See note on 226.

The usual wedding ceremony, in which the bride was escorted to the groom's house, has of course been reversed: Jason has moved into the Princess' home.

- What reason do you think Creon would have for making a marriage alliance with Jason?

312 Please: Medea enforces her plea with the ritual gesture (see note on 57), and the metre of the Greek text suggests an emotional quaver. It is to this plea that she refers in line 315.

318 my children: The importance which Creon attaches to his children relates to a central theme of the play. Notice how Medea picks the point up (332–3).

319 love: Medea means 'passionate love' (Greek *eros*). (See note on 7.)

Stichomythia (312–28)

In tragedies there are often passages of single-line dialogue (*stichomythia*). This offers an opportunity to change the pace and intensity of a scene, to create conflict and explore the relationship of the two speakers.

- In this exchange how do Creon and Medea relate to one another? Are there times when they seem to follow independent trains of thought?

You simply gave your daughter to the man of your choice.
It is my husband that I hate. What you did, I think,
Was prudent. I do not grudge you your success.
Let them marry, and good luck to you! But allow me   300
To live in Corinth. I have been wronged, but I will say
No more. You are the stronger, I am beaten.

CREON You sound harmless, but in your heart
I'm terrified you're plotting evil.
I trust you now even less than before.   305
A passionate woman – or a man, for that matter –
Is easier to guard against, than one who's clever,
And holds her tongue.
You must leave, quickly! No more talk!
It's decided. No skill of yours will help   310
You, now you are my enemy, to stay in Corinth.

MEDEA Please! I touch your knees, I beseech you
By your daughter, the new bride.

CREON You are wasting words. You'll never win me over.

MEDEA Will you banish me, and not respect my prayers?   315

CREON I'll not put you before my family.

MEDEA Oh, my fatherland! How well I now remember you!

CREON After my children, my country is my dearest love.

MEDEA Oh, what a great evil love can be for us.

CREON That depends, I'd say, on circumstances.   320

323 we need no more: Medea seems to make a disconcerting joke, implying that Creon had asked her to shoulder his burden for him.

325: Medea's words suggest that Creon's attendants approach her.

329 one day!: The action of a tragedy was often confined to a single day.

Creon's capitulation

Creon offers the second example of Medea's powers of persuasion (see page 16). He insists that he will not bow to pressure (314), but by line 338 Medea has succeeded. He is wary of her cleverness (273, 307) yet, for all her words of weakness, she gets the better of the 'stronger' party (302).

- How does this happen?
- Is Medea's behaviour spontaneous or calculated?

Note the references to physical contact (312, 324, 328 and 357).

- At line 355 Medea says she 'fawned on Creon'. What do you think she means?
- Experiment with ways of playing this scene, especially lines 312–35, to explore Medea's behaviour and chart Creon's capitulation.

Creon – tyrant?

'Tyrant' in the fifth century BC meant, simply, an autocratic ruler, and Creon may here (335) simply mean that he does not enjoy his kingly responsibility. However, the Athenians, having expelled a tyrant to establish their democracy, tended to use the word in a hostile sense (for example the Chorus in Sophocles' *Oedipus the King* say 'Pride breeds the tyrant'). Tyrants in some plays (Pentheus in *Bacchae*, Creon in *Antigone*) behave in an inflexible, despotic way, and suffer for it.

- What impression do we get of Creon from his banishment of Medea and the children, and his justification for it?

Creon's exit

- What does Creon's last sentence tell us about his state of mind?

The Chorus, to judge from their next words, do not see any great benefit in Creon's concession. Medea apparently does not show the satisfaction which she must feel at this success.

- Try ways of staging Creon's final speech and exit, to highlight his predicament, Medea's silent satisfaction and the Chorus' concern (expressed in their next speech).

MEDEA Zeus, mark who caused these troubles.

CREON Go, foolish woman, and free me of this burden.

MEDEA It is we who have the burdens; we need no more.

CREON My men will forcibly eject you.

MEDEA No, not that! I beg you, Creon, … 325

CREON It seems, madam, that you'll make it difficult.

MEDEA I'll go. I am not begging to stay.

CREON Then why struggle? Let go my hand!

MEDEA Just one day! Let me stay to make plans for our exile,

A proper start for my boys, since their father 330

No longer chooses to provide for them.

Have pity on them. You too are a father,

And should be sympathetic. I do not care about myself

In exile, but I weep for their plight.

CREON It's not my nature to be a tyrant. 335

My concern for others has often cost me dearly.

Now too, madam, I see I'm making a mistake,

But, still, I grant you your request. But I warn you,

If tomorrow's light of day sees you and your children

Within the borders of this land, 340

You die. That is my solemn, final word.

Now, if you must stay, stay one more day.

That's not long enough for you

To do the damage that I fear.

347 What welcome … ?: The Chorus refer to the network of guest-friends in the ancient world (see note on page 42). Their concern about a place of refuge unwittingly anticipates Medea's next task.

Scheming revenge

In lines 104 and 153 Medea uttered anguished cries, wishing that her sons and Jason and his new bride were dead. Here (361) her language is different – that of a cold, conscious intent to murder – and the three victims (which now include Creon but not her sons) are listed dispassionately. Notice the frequency of the word 'schemes' and associated ideas in this section. In lines 390–1 the juxtaposition of words ('Medea, Scheme and plot!') highlights the fact that the root of Medea's name (*mēd-*) is associated with plotting.

O If you were directing this play, and the actor playing Medea wanted to know exactly when Medea conceived the idea of the killings, what would you say?

371 give my enemies the laugh: In Sophocles' *Ajax*, Athena says to Ajax 'What could be sweeter than laughing at one's enemies'. But Ajax, like any epic hero, concerned for his honour, dreaded being laughed at. In her fear of mockery (expressed again in this speech in line 393, and no fewer than six times in the play, see Index), and in other ways, Medea resembles Ajax and heroes in other plays by Sophocles. (See note on page 56.)

Is Medea a witch?

373 I'll poison them: Medea is skilled in the use of *pharmaka* (herbs, drugs, potions and ointments) which have been used universally over the centuries, not only in Greek folklore. They are used in love charms, in spells, in curses, for paying off scores, and are part of other simple country 'magic'. These skills were practised usually by women and, where poison was involved, they were feared: hence Creon calls them 'evil' (273). Such women may be called 'witches', but there was no equivalent in the Greek world of the medieval witch who was associated with the Devil.

Medea was related to Circe (her father's sister, whom Homer calls a goddess), who with her drugs and wand turned Odysseus' men into pigs (*Odyssey x*). But there is no mention of Circe in this play.

The Chorus' reaction

O In view of their words when we next hear them speak (Choral Ode, 399–424), try to stage a convincing way of representing their immediate response to lines 361–3.

CHORUS Poor woman! The sadness of your plight! 345
Where can you turn?
What welcome will you find, what house
Or land to protect you from your troubles?
What an impassable sea of troubles, Medea,
God has launched you on! 350
MEDEA I am beset by troubles. Who can deny it?
But all's not over, do not think it.
There are still trials ahead for the newly wedded pair
And for those who made the marriage trouble in plenty.
Do you think I would have fawned on Creon 355
Except to win some profit in my schemes?
I would not have spoken to him – nor touched him.
But he is such a fool that,
When he could have arrested all my plans
By banishing me, he has allowed me 360
To stay this one day, in which three of my enemies
I'll send to their death –
The father, the daughter and my husband.
I have many paths to bring them death:
I do not know which first to try, my friends. 365
Shall I set fire to the bridal home,
Or drive a sharp sword through their hearts,
Creeping into their house, to where they have their bed?
There is one obstacle. If I am caught
Scheming and breaking into the house, 370
I shall be put to death and give my enemies the laugh.
The direct way is best, the one at which
I am most skilled: I'll poison them.

346–374 So … : Medea is brought back to the practical problem already foreseen by the Chorus. Note that, despite the shortness of her reprieve, she optimistically hopes for some saviour to appear. Note also that her objection to the sword (that she might be caught before she could use it) is forgotten (381) when she contemplates it a second time.
● Can you suggest reasons for this change of attitude?

375 friend: See note on guest-friends on page 42.

Medea's speech to the Chorus
In this speech Medea, alone with the Chorus, exploits her remarkable command of language (see note on Rhetoric, page 30).
● What do we learn of her qualities and emotions?
○ Explore ways of bringing out fully the speech's dramatic power.

383 Hecate: Hecate was originally a fertility goddess but she acquired many functions over the ages. Her statue stood outside all Athenian homes and she was important to women, especially at childbirth. That is how she is referred to in extant sources of Euripides' time. It is hard to know the stages by which her cult developed associations with the dead, crossroads, magic and the moon. To Medea she is of especial importance: she has set up Hecate's shrine in the centre of her household.

394 Sisyphus: He was a Corinthian hero and, in myth, a cunning rascal who was punished in Hades for some unknown sin. His punishment was to push a boulder uphill which, at the top, always slipped back. Here he is treated as the founder of the royal dynasty.

Misogyny?
397 We may not … achieve nobility: The underlying sense is that, as a woman, Medea cannot triumph by physical valour (as a hero might), but must resort to cunning. At 396 Medea may turn from addressing herself and speak to the Chorus.

Medea has, up to Creon's entry, been presented sympathetically as a vulnerable woman. But her past life, and the Nurse's hints of animal violence lurking inside her, suggest that she is no ordinary woman. Here (398) she acknowledges the evil craftiness which Creon feared (273), saying she shares it with other women (compare 254).

In a culture in which the ideal for women (as given to Athenian war widows by their leader Pericles) was to be 'the least talked of among the men whether for good or for bad' (Thucydides Book ii), a playwright who presented a bold and complex character like Medea was likely to provoke controversy, enmity and charges of misogyny.

Those wishing to discuss Euripides' own views on women can, in fact, find passages in *Medea* to support the view both that he was a proto-feminist and a misogynist.

So: suppose them dead. What state will take me in?
What friend will offer me his land as refuge, 375
A safe home, and so protect me?
There is no one. So I'll wait a little longer.
And if some tower of salvation appears,
I will pursue this murder by craft and stealth.
But if I'm driven out by events I can't control, 380
I'll take a sword, even if I risk my own death,
And kill them. I shall take the bold path of daring.
For by Queen Hecate, whom above all
I worship and have chosen as my partner,
Lodged in the inmost corner of my home, 385
I swear that none of them shall cause me grief
And not regret it. A baneful, bitter wedding
It will prove, bitter the marriage –
And my banishment!
On then! Spare none of your skill, Medea, 390
Scheme and plot! Go boldly into danger!
Now is the testing of your mettle.
You see how they treat you. You must not give the laugh
To the tribe of Sisyphus, Jason's new family by marriage.
You are of noble birth, descended from the Sun God. 395
Think on that. But we are women too:
We may not have the means to achieve nobility;
Our cleverness lies in crafting evil.

FIRST CHORAL ODE (FIRST *STASIMON*) (399–424)

This formal ode, composed of two pairs of verses, was sung with dance in the *orchēstra*. (The Chorus' first song, at their entry, was the *parodos* 121–202.) As often in tragedy, it brings together in lyric form themes from the preceding section of the play and explores the moral issues involved.

Woman power

The opening image anticipates a cosmic upheaval, a complete overthrow of established values. A new age is dawning for women. Men have always behaved as badly as women, but their misdeeds have not been recorded in song – until now.

In the second pair of verses the Chorus sympathise with Medea's situation, conscious of all her losses. They see her plight in the context of a universal moral crisis which men's faithlessness has created.

The ode contains a range of dynamics and emotion. Its dramatic power would be greatly enhanced by appropriate music and movement. The Chorus have approved the idea of Medea seeking revenge (255), and clearly in this ode they are exultant. They speak of Jason's broken oaths, but make no reference to Medea's plan.

- How would you explain this?
○ Analyse the ode, from the exultation of its explosive beginning, and suggest ways of expressing its shifting moods.

406 age-old songs: There are of course noble women in the earliest literature, like Penelope and Andromache; but women were often regarded as the source of evil, and characters like Helen of Troy and Clytemnestra were shown in a bad light. Although there *were* women poets – Corinna, Sappho, Praxilla, Telesilla – none achieved wide celebrity. The Chorus' point is that until now it is male poets who have determined values and given women a bad reputation.

408 Apollo was a god of prophecy, with oracles at Delphi and in Asia Minor; and patron of medicine, archery and music.

419 Gone is the sanctity of oaths: The Chorus relate Jason's faithlessness (also 402, and Medea, 471) to a general moral decline. The play was written at the outbreak of the war which was to involve the whole Greek world for nearly thirty years. Thucydides, the contemporary historian of the war, wrote, 'Society became divided into camps, in which no man trusted his fellow. There was neither promise to be depended upon, nor oath that could command respect.'

420 Hellas is the Greek name of Greece.

422 anchorage in distress: See notes on 156, 266.

CHORUS   Sacred rivers flow uphill:
Justice and all things are reversed.   400
It's men who are the traitors now.
There's no more faith in oaths sworn to the gods,
Our reputation will be turned to good,
We women shall have honour,
And ugly slander hold us down no more.   405

No more we'll hear the age-old songs
Celebrating women's faithlessness.
Till now Apollo, lord of song, has not bestowed
The gift of inspired lyric song
On women's minds; or we'd have echoed back a hymn   410
Against the race of men. The length of time
Has many tales to tell of men as well as women.

You sailed from your ancestral home
Crazed by love, past Pontus' twin rocks.
Now in a strange land you live   415
Husbandless, no partner in your bed;
And from this land you are driven out,
An exile without rights.

Gone is the sanctity of oaths, all sense of shame
Has left Great Hellas and flown away.   420
You do not have your father's home
To offer anchorage in distress.
Another princess rules your husband's bed,
The mistress of the house.

SECOND EPISODE (425–608)

This is the first of three confrontations between Jason and Medea.

Jason's character

Jason belongs traditionally to the world of heroic saga, of adventure and romance. The tragic playwrights used heroic tales but felt free to create their own versions of the characters – often with qualities and attitudes familiar in the 'modern' democratic Athens. In Aristophanes' *Frogs*, Euripides is criticised for presenting 'heroes' not as exemplary supermen, but with the failings of ordinary, even disreputable, mortals in real-life situations.

- How would you describe Jason in his opening speech to Medea?
- Which words in particular reveal his attitudes?

Rhetoric

The art of speaking was highly valued by the Greeks. Rhetorical skills, practised in court, in public debate and on the stage, were taught and cultivated to such an extent that people became aware of the danger of good speakers (see 557–60). Attention was paid to the structure of speeches (balancing, contrasting, numbering points and arguments; repetition of words; working up to an emotional ending) and the introduction of variety and 'drama', by means of imaginary debate, the use of 'rhetorical' questions or addressing oneself or someone absent.

Such rhetorical devices are evident in the following confrontation between Medea and Jason. They can also be found in Medea's speech to the Chorus (351–98).

Confrontation (*agōn*)

The following pair of speeches (444–98, 501–52) form a sort of debate (*agōn*), taken into Greek drama from the law court. Medea's speech resembles that of a prosecutor – hence the detailed description of her services to Jason. Notice the reference to possible witnesses (455).

The two speeches reveal much about the characters of Medea and Jason; about the balance of power in their relationship; their contrasting attitudes and values; and their response to the dramatic situation.

JASON This is not the first time, I have often realised   425
   What a train of trouble a churlish temper brings!
   You could have stayed here, kept your home,
   If you'd accepted without fuss the decision of our rulers.
   But, because of your stupid talk, you are banished.
   But it doesn't bother me. Go on calling me   430
   The vilest names you like.
   But after what you said about the royal family,
   Consider yourself lucky that your punishment
   Is merely exile. They are furious.
   I've tried to calm their royal temper. I wanted you to stay.   435
   But you go on being foolish, endlessly
   Abusing your masters, and so you're banished.
   Despite all this, I don't let down my friends.
   I've come, thinking of your needs, my dear: I wouldn't want
   You sent away with the children penniless   440
   Or lacking anything. Exile brings with it
   Many problems. Even if you hate me,
   I could never wish you harm.
MEDEA You vile coward! Yes, I can call you that,
   The worst name that I know for your unmanliness!   445
   You've come to me, you, my worst enemy, come here?
   But that's not bravery or courage, to betray your loved ones,
   Then look them in the eye.
   It's utter shamelessness,
   The worst disease that mankind suffers.   450
   However – you've done well to come.
   Abusing you will do me good
   And you will smart to hear it.

455–66: For events at Colchis and Iolcus, see Background to the story, page v.

460: Note that Medea does not mention here the murder of her brother Apsyrtus. But she does not hide or diminish her role in the murder of Pelias.

● Can you suggest any reasons for this?

Medea is accusing Jason of ingratitude.

● How else may her words affect our view of Jason?

Diana Rigg as Medea, Almeida Theatre production, 1992.

472 the gods by whom we swore: Medea never loses her conviction of the rightness of her case, which is based on Jason's faithlessness. She confidently appeals to the gods – specifically Zeus (see 495, compare 321).

Medea's 'masculine' language

478 I'll deal with you: Medea's language and style are that of a practised lawyer. In the confident and skilful way in which she handles arguments, her use of rhetoric, her wrestling metaphor (563) and reference to military life (239), and the sophistic skill with which she deals with Creon (notes on pages 18 and 22) she shows a familiarity with the man's world. (See also note on page 56.)

I will begin at the beginning.
I saved your life – as those Greeks know, 455
Who sailed with you in the *Argo*,
When you were sent to yoke the fire-breathing bulls
And sow the field of death. It was I who killed
The sleepless serpent, which within its tangled coils
Guarded the Golden Fleece. I lit the way 460
For your escape.
I betrayed my father and my home.
With you I went to Iolcus under Pelion,
With more loyalty than sense. I killed
King Pelias – an agonising death 465
At his own daughters' hands – and destroyed his whole house.
All this I did for you. And you, foulest of men,
Have betrayed me. You have got another woman,
When I have borne you sons. If you had no children,
This lusting for her might have been forgiven. 470
Gone is all faith in oaths. I don't understand –
Can you really think the gods by whom we swore
No longer rule? Or that now there is a new ordinance for men,
When you know you have betrayed your promises to me?
My poor hand, which you so often clasped, 475
And knees you touched in supplication:
All false! My hopes dashed by a traitor!
But, come, I'll deal with you as if you were a friend –
Though what good do I think I'll get from you?
Still, if you answer me, you'll show yourself in yet baser light: 480
Where can I now turn? To my father's home, my country,
Which I betrayed when I came here?

485 I am now an enemy: Medea is as much an enemy to her family in Colchis as Jason is to his.

Medea's speech
- What devices of rhetoric (see note on page 30) do you find in Medea's speech? Does it reveal new qualities?
- Does the speech increase your understanding of her or your sympathy for her?

Jason's reply
Note the formality and artifice of the beginning of Jason's reply (501–3).
- How systematic and structured is his defence?
- What answers does he offer to Medea's charges?
- Is there more evidence of rhetorical polish in Jason's speech than Medea's?
- What devices of the orator do you notice?

497–8 no stamp/To show our worth: This is not the only place in Euripides' plays that the wish is expressed that we could know a person's real character. It occurs when a character experiences or suspects dishonesty or artifice. Yet Medea's protest to Zeus is itself a trick of rhetoric, a form of artifice.

Our word 'character' comes from the Greek *charaktēr*, originally an image stamped on a coin to show its value.

502 with sail tight-furled: In stormy weather sailors rolled the sail and secured it to the 'yard' to reduce the sail area.

507–8 Eros/With his … darts: Eros (Cupid) was originally an independent god of love; in later mythology he was the attendant or son of Aphrodite (Venus), either of whose arrows could compel a person to fall in love. It is a traditional part of the legend that Hera asked Aphrodite to make Medea fall in love with Jason.

To play down Medea's part in his escape from Colchis, Jason reminds Medea of this. But, in the eyes of the Greeks, divine prompting seems to have done nothing to lessen mortals' credit or guilt for their actions.
- What does this tell us about Jason?

Or to Pelias' wretched daughters? A fine welcome
They would give me, who killed their father.
The fact is, to my loved ones at home I am now an enemy: 485
Those to whom I should have done no harm
Are – because I supported you – my sworn enemies.
As my reward, you made me seem fortunate indeed
In many Greek women's eyes! But what a marvellous husband
I have! So loyal and true! I shall be cast out, 490
An exile bereft of friends, alone and lonely
With your sons. That's a fine reproach you take
Into your new marriage, that your sons and I,
Who saved your life, are beggars on the road!
Zeus, you granted men sure signs to tell 495
When gold is counterfeit. But when we need to tell
Which men are false, why do our bodies bear no stamp
To show our worth?

CHORUS Anger is fearful and hard to heal,
When those who once were lovers start to fight. 500

JASON I must, I think, show that I am no bad speaker,
And, like a careful helmsman, with sail tight-furled,
Ride out the tempest of your stinging tongue, my dear.
You build up your services to me; but I consider
That my only guardian on my travels, god or man, 505
Was Aphrodite, she alone. You have a subtle mind,
But the unpalatable truth is it was Eros
With his inescapable darts who drove you
To save my life.
But I'll not make too fine a point of that. 510

Greeks and barbarians

514–16 the country that you left is primitive …: Jason calls Medea's country 'barbarian', a word originally used for people who did not speak Greek. The Greeks, though prepared to admire some qualities in such people, nevertheless generally felt superior. They were free, whereas barbarians were 'slaves'. Even if he did not live in a democracy, in which he had a share in government, a Greek was a 'member' of his *polis*, not a subject; he was ruled by Law, whereas the barbarian was seen to live at the mercy of arbitrary despots.

Jason depicts Medea as a primitive foreigner, faced by the civilised, rational values of the Greek world.

● How well do Jason – and the Corinthian state – represent these values?

521 Orpheus: Orpheus was said to be the son of one of the Muses and was the most celebrated musician of legend. He was so skilful that, by his singing, he could charm wild beasts and stop rivers flowing.

Jason's motivation

525–44 what I've done is wise: Jason's argument in the following section might not have surprised the predominantly (or possibly exclusively) male audience in Athens. There full citizenship was, after 451 BC, denied to children who could not prove that both their parents were full citizens. By distancing himself from a foreign, non-Greek wife, and by allying himself to the ruling family, Jason could have been seen to be helping his sons.

Jason insists (533, 573) that he is not in love with the Princess. (For Medea's view, see 604.)

● Do you believe Jason?

527 Keep quiet!: Jason's claim that he is acting out of love for his sons seems to provoke some response from Medea.

531 marry the king's daughter: Does the irony of this not occur to Jason? This is exactly what he did to extricate himself from trouble at Colchis.

What help you gave me I am grateful for.
But in return for saving me, you gained
More than you gave, as I will demonstrate.
First: the country that you left is primitive, but now
You live in Greece. You now know what Justice means,   515
Enjoy the benefits of Law, not the rule of force.
All Greece has come to know your talents: you are famous.
If you still lived at the end of the world,
No one would mention you. As far as I'm concerned,
I wouldn't pray for gold or skill   520
To sing better than Orpheus, if these did not
Bring me celebrity.
So much about my exploits, in answer to your challenge.
As for your spiteful words about my marriage with the princess,
I'll show that what I've done is wise and prudent;   525
And I've acted out of love for you
And for *my* sons. Keep quiet!
When I moved here from Iolcus
With a trail of problems and misfortune,
What more lucky chance could I meet with,   530
As an exile, than to marry the king's daughter?
It's not – as you are galled to think – that I am tired
Of your bed or smitten with desire for my new bride –
Nor keen to be a champion at fathering many sons.
The children which we have are enough. I have no complaint.   535

Jason's values

Jason reveals a lot about his values and priorities.

● What do we learn of his attitude to marriage and children; to his own wife and sons; to loyalty; to money and possessions; to social status, especially the royal family; to exile and his present plight?

● To what extent do these differ from Medea's values?

● Do you assume that Jason is totally sincere?

Both the Chorus (553) and Medea (557) suggest that Jason has made a plausible speech, as he had hoped to (501). (See note on 525–44.)

○ Attempt a performance which would show Jason in the most favourable light.

The *agōn*

● Does the *agōn* (debate) present a contrast between a male and female view of life?

● How important is it that Jason is a Greek and Medea a 'barbarian'?

● How much do the characters of Medea and Jason colour what they say?

After the two long speeches the *agōn* is continued in shorter, passionate exchanges (556–608).

My chief wish was that we should live well
And not be poor – friends vanish when one's poor –
And that I could bring up the boys in a manner
Worthy of my family; and, if I did have other sons,
I could join them as brothers with my sons by you,   540
And, uniting the family together, I could prosper.
What need have you of more children? But it makes sense
For me to gain advantages for those we already have
By means of those to come. Is that such a bad idea?
You wouldn't say so, if you weren't sexually jealous.   545
You go so far, you women, as to think
That if all's well in bed, your life's complete.
But if your sex life goes wrong,
All that was best and beautiful you make a battle field.
Man should have found some other way   550
To procreate. The female sex should not exist:
Then we'd be free of all our troubles.
CHORUS Jason, you have put a fine gloss on your words.
But – I may not be wise to say this – I think
You've acted wrongly: you have betrayed your wife.   555
MEDEA I differ from many people in many ways.
To me, an unjust man who is also clever with words
Deserves the greatest penalty.
Confident that he can dress up his wrongdoing
With specious words, he is brazen in his wickedness.   560
And yet he is not so clever after all.

563 One point will floor you: Metaphors from wrestling were common in legal language. (See note on 478.)

● Why would this argument 'floor' Jason?

Medea and the boys, Almeida Theatre production, 1992.

So don't you try your plausible and clever arguments on me!
One point will floor you: if you'd been honourable,
You should have won me over before you married,
Not kept it from your loved ones! 565

JASON I'm sure that if I had announced my wedding plans,
You would have been most helpful!
Even now you can't bring yourself to give up
The great bitterness you feel.

MEDEA That is not what stopped you. You thought, 570
As you grew older, it didn't look quite right
To have a foreign wife.

JASON Get this straight: it is not for any woman
That I made this royal marriage. I've already said
I did it to safeguard you, to father royal sons, 575
Brothers to my children, a security for my house.

MEDEA I want none of your hurtful 'prosperity'
Or wealth to rankle in my mind.

JASON You'd better change your attitude. You'll be wiser
To accept what's best for you is not 'hurtful'. 580
You're fortunate. Don't think you're not.

MEDEA That's right, insult me! You have a way out.
I am alone, condemned to exile.

JASON It was your own choice. Blame no one else.

585 Did I make you my wife …?: Medea's language, which highlights the different status of man and wife, is disconcerting, as is her next line 'I am that curse'. Jason breaks off the dialogue (589).

Guest-friends

In the dangerous world of the early Greeks, rich and powerful men established networks of guest-friends. They formed ties – bonds of trust – with their peers around the Greek world. These ties committed them to provide one another with hospitality and shelter when travelling, help with provisions, servants and support in cases of emergency. These were contracts between individuals, which often passed to succeeding generations of their families. Some such help as Jason offers Medea (593, 596) would have been essential for her when travelling.

595 It will pay you: The metaphor is appropriate for someone who mentions money so often (see Index – Money).

599 I call the Gods to witness: Medea has already (472) told Jason that he has no understanding of the way in which the gods work. Here he continues to call on their aid.

604 You're lusting: Jason three times taunts Medea with references to 'bed' or 'sex' (*lekhos* 533, 545, 547), suggesting that what irks her is the thought that he prefers the Princess to her.
- Does this final jibe of Medea's suggest that Jason is right?
- Try ways of staging this scene (556–608) to bring out the intensity of the emotions.

MEDEA What have I done? Did I make you my wife   585
  And then betray you?

JASON You called down unholy curses on the royal family.

MEDEA I am that curse, to your house too.

JASON I won't debate this further. If you need
  Money for the children or yourself,   590
  To support you in exile, let me know.
  I am happy to give, generously – and to send
  Letters of introduction to my guest-friends,
  Who will treat you well. You will be foolish, my dear,
  To refuse. It will pay you to give up your anger.   595

MEDEA I would not take advantage of your friends
  Or accept a thing. Don't try to give me anything!
  There can be no profit in a traitor's gift.

JASON Then I call the Gods to witness that I am willing
  To do any service for you and for the boys.   600
  But you do not want kindness:
  In your stubborn pride you reject your dear ones
  And make your suffering worse.

MEDEA Go! You're lusting for your new-won bride,
  Lingering here, away from the house!   605
  Go to her bed!
  Perhaps – with a god's help, it will be said – this marriage
  Will be celebrated with a funeral dirge!

SECOND CHORAL ODE (2ND *STASIMON*) (609–39)

As in the first ode, the Chorus reflect on the developments of the preceding scene. They recoil from any form of excess (like the Nurse, 118).

The Nurse at the beginning of the play (7) described Medea's love in strong terms. Here the Chorus sing of the damage which both excessive and adulterous love can cause.

In the second pair of verses they identify with Medea's plight: homeless, isolated, betrayed. Again (see 347, 421) they comment on her lack of friends or refuge.

- What is the tone of this ode? How does it differ from that of the first ode?

625 exile: The Greek word is *apolis* – 'stateless' – expressing the worst aspect of exile (see note on line 244).

Staging the ode

Medea remains on stage when Jason leaves at the end of the preceding scene. In the Classical theatre, it is not certain that she would acknowledge the Chorus' words.

- Suppose that she did react: think of her feelings, and how she would behave. Would the Chorus women keep a respectful distance or would they approach her?
- Would it be effective to allocate lines to individuals?
- What sort of music would be appropriate?

CHORUS	When love overwhelms a man,	
	It can destroy his virtue	610
	And his good name.	
	But love in moderation –	
	No other God can bring such blessing.	
	Aphrodite, never point at me your golden bow,	
	Tainting with desire your arrow	615
	Which none can avoid.	

When love overwhelms a man,
It can destroy his virtue   610
And his good name.
But love in moderation –
No other God can bring such blessing.
Aphrodite, never point at me your golden bow,
Tainting with desire your arrow   615
Which none can avoid.

Moderation is what I want:
That is the Gods' best gift.
May dread Love not excite me for another's bed,
Causing angry quarrels   620
And unending strife.
May Aphrodite respect harmonious love
And know good wives from bad.

Oh, my country, my home!
May I never be an exile,   625
Living a life of helpless wandering,
Of the most pitiable grief.
I would rather die, die,
Than live to see that day.
No torment can be worse   630
Than losing your homeland.

We see it. It is not hearsay
That we reflect upon.
Your suffering is terrible,
Yet no state, no friend ,shows pity.   635
A thankless death to anyone
Who has unlocked the pure heart
Of one who is dear and then dishonours her!
He'll be no friend of ours.

THIRD EPISODE (640–802)

Just when Medea needs to find a place of refuge Aegeus, king of
Athens, arrives to provide one. Aristotle, in his treatise *The Art of
Poetry*, found this improbable (*alogon*), saying also that no use is made
of the character. (See note on page 52.)

- What does Euripides achieve by the use of *stichomythia* (see page
  20) in lines 644–84?
- What does it help to reveal about the two characters?

644 Phoebus' ancient oracle: To the Greeks, Delphi was the centre of
the world. It was also the site of the oracle of Phoebus Apollo, which
was still consulted in Euripides' day on a wide range of problems. That
Aegeus went there shows how seriously he regarded his plight. (See
note on The importance of sons, page 6.)

653 May I know …?: Medea is scrupulous to make sure there is no
impediment to her being told the god's reply.

660 Pittheus: See note on 694–6.

AEGEUS Medea, I wish you joy! There is no better way   640
   To greet a friend.

MEDEA And joy to you, Aegeus, son of wise Pandion!
   Where are you travelling from?

AEGEUS From Phoebus' ancient oracle.

MEDEA Earth's prophetic centre. What took you there?   645

AEGEUS To enquire how I may beget children.

MEDEA Indeed! At your age are you still childless?

AEGEUS We are. Some spirit seems to will it.

MEDEA You have a wife?

AEGEUS I am married.   650

MEDEA And what did Phoebus say about children?

AEGEUS Words too subtle for a man to interpret.

MEDEA May I know the god's reply?

AEGEUS Indeed! A clever mind is what we need.

MEDEA What did he say? Come, tell me, since you may.   655

AEGEUS 'Do not unstop the wineskin's neck …'

MEDEA Until you do what or go where?

AEGEUS Until I am back in my ancestral home.

MEDEA Then why take ship for Corinth?

AEGEUS You know of Pittheus, King of Troezen …   660

MEDEA Pelops' son. They say he is very pious.

664 spear-friends: The word is used by the tragedians to describe kings or chiefs in armed alliance with one another.

665 I wish you success: Medea does not at this stage offer help to Aegeus. She seems to close the subject of his childlessness. Then (666) Aegeus notices Medea's distress.
- What is the effect of her use of his name (667)?

676 let him go: Aegeus seems to treat Jason's betrayal of Medea as merely unfortunate, until he realises that he has abandoned her for another marriage.

AEGEUS I want to talk to him about the oracle.

MEDEA He is wise, and expert in these matters.

AEGEUS Yes, and dearest to me of all my spear-friends.

MEDEA Then I wish you success in what you seek.   665

AEGEUS You look unhappy. Your cheeks are wasted.

MEDEA Aegeus, I have the worst husband on earth.

AEGEUS What? You are depressed. Explain.

MEDEA Jason has betrayed me, but I have done him no wrong.

AEGEUS What has he done? Tell me more clearly.   670

MEDEA He's made another woman mistress of the house – over me!

AEGEUS He wouldn't dare! That's disgraceful!

MEDEA He has. Those he loved he treats with utter disrespect.

AEGEUS Is he in love with her? Or out of love with you?

MEDEA Oh, it's a mighty passion! No loyalty to those he should love.   675

AEGEUS Then let him go – if he is the villain that you say.

MEDEA What he's set his heart on is a royal marriage.

AEGEUS Who is the girl's father? Go on!

MEDEA The King of Corinth, Creon.

AEGEUS Then, lady, I fully understand your grief.   680

MEDEA I am ruined. What's more, I'm banished.

AEGEUS By whom? Worse and worse!

685 he will put up with it: This seems to be a wry joke.

687 by your knees I beseech you: The Greek words, as when Medea appealed to Creon, suggest an emotional quaver. (See note on 312.)

691–2 So may the gods …: This is a formula which we have in oaths ('… so help me God'). If Aegeus helps Medea, she is asking that the gods in return help him. Notice how it is not until she has fully engaged Aegeus' sympathy that Medea offers to help him, linking the offer to her need for asylum. (See note on 665.)

694–6 I will put an end …: The common version of the story was that Aegeus visited Pittheus to consult him about the oracle. Pittheus understood its meaning – that Aegeus was to refrain from drink till he reached Athens. But, not telling this to Aegeus, he got him drunk and put him to bed with his daughter Aethra. As a result, she became mother of Theseus, who was to be the greatest Athenian hero. Euripides has added to the story the meeting of Aegeus and Medea, and her offer of help. Her ability to arrange the help is not in question.

698 for the gods' sake: Aegeus acknowledges the obligation which Medea has put upon him by her ritual entreaty.

699: Aegeus finds a decorous way of referring to his impotence.

701 patron (*proxenos*): A *proxenos* looked after the interests of foreign citizens. (See note on Guest-friends on page 42.)

704 By your own devices: Medea has a place of asylum, but how she is to get there is still to be decided.

Aegeus' oath
Aegeus has offered asylum without knowing Medea's intentions. She wants this confirmed by an oath (713–17), which he trustingly gives.
- Is Medea abusing Aegeus and the sanctity of oaths?
- How would you stage this, to highlight its significance?

MEDEA Creon has banished me from Corinth.

AEGEUS And Jason permits this? How despicable.

MEDEA He says not, but he will put up with it. 685
Aegeus, I beg you, by your beard
And by your knees I beseech you, pity,
Have pity on me in my misfortune.
Do not watch me cast out, destitute.
Give me shelter in Athens, in your home. 690
So may the gods fulfil your wish for children,
And you yourself die happy.
You do not know what lucky chance
You have met with here. I will put an end
To your lack of children, make sure you beget 695
Offspring. I know potions for that.

AEGEUS For many reasons I am keen to help you,
Lady: for the gods' sake, and the promise of children.
For this my own powers seem quite spent …
This is the situation: if you can come to my land 700
I shall try to honour my duties as your patron.
But I must make it plain: I will not take you
With me from Corinth. If you come to my home
By your own devices, you shall have sanctuary.
I will not give you up to anyone. But you must 705
Leave Corinth on your own. I have friends here too.
I don't want them to blame me.

MEDEA It shall be so. If I could have some pledge from you,
All would be fine.

AEGEUS Do you not trust me? What worries you? 710

MEDEA I do trust you. But I have enemies – the house
Of Pelias, and Creon here.
If you were bound by oath, you would not give me up
Or let them abduct me from your country.

Aegeus' oath

724: Medea makes Aegeus swear by Earth and Sun, who have been invoked before, in association with Zeus (137). They are also mentioned at significant moments later in the play (see Index).

725 And all the race of Gods: This phrase is regularly added at the end of prayers, as a precaution, in case the person praying has offended a god by omitting him or her.

732 if you break your oath: Aegeus accepts that breaking one's oath is a sin and must be punished. Medea knows she is dealing with a pious man, unlike Jason (compare 1371–2).

In the *Iliad*, Agamemnon makes a similar solemn oath: 'Be Zeus my witness and Earth and Sun and the Erinyes, who under the earth take vengeance on those who swear a false oath, that I ... And, if anything of this oath be false, may the gods give me all the woes that they give to him who sins against them in his oath.' Note the formula, and the punishments which would follow perjury.

738 Hermes: Hermes is the messenger of the gods. He guides the dead to Hades and looks after travellers and merchants.

740 Aegeus' exit: Aegeus says no farewell. Has he abandoned his trip to Pittheus?
- Do the Chorus imply (738) that he is going straight home?

The character of Aegeus
- From the evidence of the scene – from what he says, the way he says it, from his behaviour, Medea's attitude to him and what the Chorus say about him, produce a character sketch of Aegeus.
- Aegeus is sometimes played as a comic character. Is there any evidence in the text to support this?
- He is trusting and generous. His lack of children takes from his dignity, so that he is extremely grateful to Medea for her offer to cure him. Does this make him gullible and an easy person for Medea to manipulate?

The scene's significance
It has been argued that the significance of the scene is not simply that Medea wins yet another (the third) favour, a place of asylum, but that her meeting with Aegeus suggests to her the idea of killing her children. The plight of Aegeus, a king without son and heir, appears – so the argument goes – so pathetic, that it suggests to Medea the perfect act of revenge on Jason.
- How convincing do you find this? Is there any evidence in the text to support it?
- What new qualities of Medea are revealed in this scene?

But if you agree in words alone, not sworn by the Gods   715
You would perhaps lend a friendly ear to their
Advances. I am weak. They have wealth and royal power.

AEGEUS In what you say, you show great foresight.
If that is what you want, I'll not refuse.
An oath will safeguard me –   720
I'll have an excuse to offer to your enemies –
And your position is stronger.
Name your Gods.

MEDEA Swear by Earth and Sun, the father of my father,
And all the race of Gods.   725

AEGEUS What shall I swear to do or not to do? You say!

MEDEA Never yourself to expel me from your land
And never, if any of my enemies wishes to take me away,
Willingly, while you live, to hand me over to them.

AEGEUS I swear by Earth, and by the Sun's bright light,   730
And all the Gods, to abide by what you say.

MEDEA Good. And if you break your oath?

AEGEUS I must suffer the fate of all sinful men.

MEDEA Go then! God speed! All's well.
I'll reach your city as soon as possible,   735
When I have done what I intend,
And achieved my wish.

CHORUS May lord Hermes, Maia's son, guide you home, Aegeus,
And may you achieve what you earnestly desire,
For you seem to me a man of noble spirit.   740

Medea's plan

Medea is exultant (741). Her invocation, involving the gods in her revenge, shows that she is confident she is in the right.

Her plan begins to take shape (see page 24). Here there is no specific mention of Creon or Jason. The focus is first on the plan to kill the Princess and whoever touches her.

Then Medea says that she will kill her children (769). This is the first time that she has revealed this.

● How long has it been in her mind? Remember the Nurse's concerns for the boys' safety (35–8) and Medea's tormented curses (104–5).

There is a reason for concentrating on the death of her sons and the Princess, which Medea is about to reveal (781–4 and 795–6). She talks of destroying the whole house (771), which she will achieve by killing the sons. (See note on The importance of sons, page 6.)

The boys are not only to die, they are also to be used to secure entry into the palace and as unwitting agents of murder.

● What is Medea's state of mind? Do we see a new side of her?

745–8 Just when I was foundering: Metaphor merges with reality: Medea imagines herself in difficulties at sea, but finding shelter at Athens.

748 Pallas' city: This is a reference to Athens, of which Pallas Athene was protector.

766 I'll anoint: By line 924, the gifts are ready and in the boys' hands. It is hard to see when Medea can leave the stage to apply the poison. She could in theory leave at line 802, but the Chorus address her at line 819. Either she is not present for the ode, even when the Chorus address her, or someone brings the gifts on stage. (Note that the Nurse seems to be present at 799.)

○ How would you solve this problem of staging?

The Chorus

Medea addresses them (742) and takes them fully into her confidence. They have thought it right for her to want revenge (255), sympathised and exulted with her (First Ode).

● How do you think they receive this speech, up to the point when Medea reveals her intention to kill the boys?

● Do you think there are details which they relish?

MEDEA Zeus, Justice, child of Zeus! Light of the Sun!
Now, my friends, I shall triumph over my enemies.
I am on my way.
Now there is hope my enemies will pay the price.
Just when I was foundering, this man   745
Has appeared, a haven for my schemes,
Where I shall find safe anchorage
When I reach Pallas' city.
Now I will tell you all my plans.
Do not expect pleasant listening.   750
I'll send a servant to ask Jason
To come to see me.
And when he comes, I'll speak submissively,
Say I agree with him: this royal marriage,
For which he has betrayed me, is fine –   755
Expedient and well-judged.
But I shall ask that my children may stay:
Not that I would leave them in a hostile land
For my enemies to abuse;
I'll use them in a plot to kill the princess.   760
I'll send them, bearing gifts to the bride,
A finely woven dress and crown of beaten gold,
Begging not to be banished from this land.
And, if she takes this finery and lets it touch her skin,
She will die horribly – and all who touch the girl.   765
With such deadly poisons I'll anoint the gifts.
That part of the plan I now leave. My heart
Cries out in grief for what must be done thereafter.
I shall kill my children.
No one shall take them from me.   770

773 The most unholy crime: The shedding of kindred blood was the worst of crimes. Medea acknowledges that infanticide is in a wholly different category from the other murders she plans. (See note on page 88.)

777 no refuge: Aegeus *has* offered her a refuge, but the refuge which Medea most longs for is Colchis, to which she can no longer return.

779 a Greek man's words:
● How important is Jason's race to Medea?

780 pay the price: The boys are to be killed because Medea thinks this will hurt Jason most (796).

787 Good to my friends: See next note, and note on Friends and enemies (page 6).

Medea's heroic qualities
788 Such people win the greatest glory: Medea shows some of the qualities associated with Homeric heroes like Achilles and Ajax, or (in some degree) characters like Ajax and Antigone in the plays of Euripides' contemporary, Sophocles. She is moved by great passions (1049), especially anger (166, etc.). She is like a wild animal (83, 179), larger than life (see note on 118), rejecting moderation (798), dangerous (37). She is full of passionate intensity (99–101), daring (830), will not be deflected from her purpose (602, 998). Above all, she is concerned for her honour (19, 32, 1333): she will not tolerate injustice or mockery (see note on 371; even preferring to kill her sons, 775) and seeks revenge for any wrong done to her (155, etc.).

798 no time for moderation: Contrast the attitude of the Nurse (see note on 118) and Chorus (617). The line helps to explain the Nurse's words 'Beware a royal temper' (110–12).

799 Go and fetch: The rest of the speech suggests this is addressed to the Nurse.
● When did she enter?

802 a woman: Medea continues to present her cause as that of all women, and expects loyalty from the Nurse and the Chorus.

The Chorus' reaction
● How do the Chorus express their disapproval of Medea's plans?
○ Explore ways of staging the scene to express Medea's terrifying intensity and the Chorus' response.

Jason's whole house I shall demolish
And leave the country, guilty of
The most unholy crime, the murder of my dearest sons.
That I can endure; but I cannot endure
The mockery of my enemies. 775
What do I care? What point is there in living? I have
No fatherland, no home, no refuge from distress.
My mistake was to desert my father's house,
Won over by a Greek man's words.
But he, with God's help, will pay the price. 780
He will never see alive again the sons
He had by me; nor will he father children
With his new bride, for by my poison she, the wretch,
Is doomed to die a wretched death.
Let no one think me weak, of no account, 785
Submissive. I am made of different stuff:
Good to my friends, but grievous to my enemies.
Such people win the greatest glory.
CHORUS Since you have confided this to us ...
We want to help you, but we can't reject 790
The laws of human life. We say,
Don't do this!
MEDEA There is no other way. I understand your saying this,
But you have not suffered as I have.
CHORUS But can you bring yourself to kill your own sons, madam? 795
MEDEA It is the way to hurt my husband most.
CHORUS And make yourself the most unhappy of women.
MEDEA What do I care? This is no time for moderation.
Go and fetch Jason.
I can put my trust in you. Say nothing 800
Of my plans, if you are loyal to your mistress –
And a woman.

THIRD CHORAL ODE (3RD *STASIMON*) (803–36)

The Chorus praise Athens in extravagant terms and ask how such a civilised state, which prides itself on offering asylum, can receive someone polluted by infanticide.

They cannot understand how Medea can bring herself to kill her sons; they dwell on the horrendous details and plead with her passionately not to do it.

Athens

The Greek for '**men of Athens**' is literally 'sons of Erechtheus'. Erechtheus was son of Earth and mythical founder of Athens. Hence the Athenians are **children of the ... gods** and their land **holy**. His temple, the *Erechtheum* (not yet built when *Medea* was first performed), still stands on the Acropolis.

Athens was the intellectual and artistic capital of the Greek world. Its climate (**clear air** – 807) was thought to contribute to the Athenians' sharp wits.

The **Muses** inspired writers and artists of all sorts. They are associated with the district of **Pieria** near Mount Olympus. In this ode they are said to bless Athens, which in Euripides' time was home to a brilliant array of poets, sculptors, architects, potters, philosophers and scientists – that is the **golden Harmony** which the Muses collectively engender.

Aphrodite is associated with Harmony and the Muses in myth and vase paintings. Here Love's agents (*Erotes* or Cupids) are said to combine with Wit to produce art of all sorts, implying that art is a blend of passion and intellect.

805 never plundered: Until the war between Athens and Sparta, which was just beginning in 431 BC (the date of *Medea*'s first production), Attica had suffered foreign occupation only for brief periods. The war eventually involved most of the Greek world and ended with Athens' humiliation in 404 BC.

810 Cephisus was one of the rivers of Athens; the river god was also an ancestor of Athens.

CHORUS The men of Athens have been fortunate of old,
    Children of the blessed gods:
   Their land is holy, never plundered,   805
    They feed on their famed wit
  And sprightly step through bright, clear air,
 Where, they say, the nine Muses of sacred Pieria
   Created golden Harmony.

   By the streams of lovely Cephisus   810
They say that Aphrodite, drawing water, breathed
 Down the valley gentle sweet-breathed airs;
   Always wearing on her hair
    A fragrant crown of roses,
  She sends young Loves to sit with Wit,   815
   Helping create their diverse arts.

The Chorus

The Chorus hardly ever interfere in the action of a Greek tragedy. (One exception is in Sophocles' *Antigone* when the Chorus tell Creon to undo his errors.) The Corinthian women are anyway bound by their promise (255) not to reveal Medea's plan, so all they can do is to try to shock her into a recognition of the enormity of what she intends to do. This they do, firstly, by setting her in the context of her place of asylum: they say she will pollute the sacred rarefied atmosphere of Athens if she takes sanctuary there. (See also note on 820 and on page 88.) Then they fall back on the hope that Medea will not be able to turn a deaf ear to her sons' entreaties.

820 Pollution in their midst: Murder was thought to confer a stain on the killer which could be cleansed only by ritual purification. This pollution was considered contagious and could affect a whole community. (For example, in Sophocles' *Oedipus Tyrannus* Oedipus' unwitting murder of his father caused a plague in Thebes.)

824 We beseech you: Medea has exploited the ritual entreaty with Creon and Aegeus, yet she herself is impervious to the Chorus' passionate appeal. Their attempts to dissuade Medea from her plan remind us of the Nurse's words (28) which likened her to a rock or wave. Jason also referred to her stubbornness (602).

o How would you stage the Chorus' appeal to Medea to bring out its irony, that now she is the object of an entreaty, and to bring out the dramatic significance?

Medea's 'fearful nerve' (830)

The Chorus highlight that quality of Medea, her 'fearful nerve' (*tolma*), to which she has herself referred (382, 'daring') – a blend of daring, ruthlessness and determination. This quality marks her out from ordinary women. (See also note on page 92 and Index.)

How can this city of sacred rivers,
A land that welcomes those it loves,
Shelter you, the child-killer,
Pollution in their midst? 820
Think about the blow you will strike
At your own sons.
Think about the murder which you plan.
We beseech you, at your knees,
Entreat and plead with you: 825
Do not kill your children.

How will you harden your heart,
Steel your mind and hand,
Summoning against your sons
Your fearful nerve? 830
How will you look on the boys,
Take on your role of murderer –
And not weep?
When your sons kneel to you for mercy,
You will not be able heartlessly 835
To bathe your hand in their blood.

FOURTH EPISODE (837–944)

840 Jason: This is the only time in the play that Medea addresses Jason by name.

- Does Medea's similar use of Aegeus' name (667) help us, right from the beginning, to establish the tone of her speech?
- Jason never addresses Medea by name, whereas both Creon and Aegeus do. Do you think this is significant?

Medea's internal debate (844–52)

In this passage Medea 'dramatises' her inner conflict.

- What are the advantages to Medea in doing this?
- Where do the arguments of her 'other self' in fact come from? Medea here exploits her acting skills. Clearly she knows Jason well enough to know how to win him over.
- What effect does this have on our attitude to her?
- Explore ways of expressing her mastery over him.

858 beside the marriage bed: It was the role of the bride's attendants (who had to be mothers) to be with her in the nuptial chamber. One would have expected the bride's mother, rather than the groom's ex-wife, to attend the bride! Possibly the line suggests that Medea is over-acting, that her 'performance' is getting out of control. (See also note on 924.)

The children

The boys enter at line 864 with the Tutor. They are the most important focus of attention in this section of the play, which the staging must reflect. (See also note on 884.)

JASON I have come, as you commanded: despite your ill-will,
I will grant you this, my dear. I'll listen to you.
What new request do you have of me?

MEDEA Jason, please forgive me for what I said.   840
You must bear with my moods – we two
Once showed such kindness to one another.
I've had some harsh words with myself:
'Fool! Why be so mad? Why resent
Those who are making sensible plans,   845
Antagonise the country's rulers and my husband?
He's doing what's in our best interest –
He's marrying a princess and fathering brothers
For my sons. Stop being angry! What's the matter with me?
The Gods are providing for us well.   850
I have the children; don't I know we're exiles
And have not many friends?'
So I reflected and I realised how stupid
I had been, how pointless my anger.
I now applaud you, think that you are right   855
In bringing us this new marriage. I was a fool.
I should have been part of your plans,
Helped you, stood beside the marriage bed,
Rejoiced to attend your new bride.
But we women, we are – I won't say 'bad', but we're –   860
What we are. You shouldn't follow our bad example,
And answer folly with folly. I ask your pardon.
I admit that I was wrong, but I've had wiser thoughts.
Children, children, come, leave the house, come out,
Embrace your father with me, talk to him,   865
With your mother end the feud and all make friends.
We've made a truce. I am no longer angry.

868 Take his right hand: Medea deliberately enacts the gesture whose associations cause her so much grief: Jason would have clasped her hand in making oaths and entreaties to her. Hence the emotional cry that follows.

873–4 tears: The use of masks did not prevent playwrights describing such physical details. (See also 892.)

884 As for you, boys: Just as Medea did (864), Jason turns and speaks directly to the boys.

○ It might be effective to highlight this symmetry in the staging. How could this be done?

Jason's response to Medea's speech

● What does Jason's reaction to Medea's speech tell us about him?
● How would you describe his attitude to Medea?
● Does Jason's speech add to our knowledge of him? In particular, do we learn more of his attitude to the boys?
● Does his speech confirm Medea's view of his values?

898 Woman is the weaker sex: The line, the culmination of her 'performance', sums up Medea's brazen artifice.

Take his right hand. Oh, I think of hidden troubles!
Children, will you live long and stretch out
Your loving arms like this? Oh dear!   870
I'm going to cry. I am full of fear.
At last I've ended my quarrel with your father –
But, look, I've drenched your darling face with tears.
CHORUS I too am weeping fresh tears.
I pray that there is no more trouble,   875
That things don't get worse.
JASON I'm glad of this, my dear.
But I don't blame you for what went before.
It is to be expected that the female sex will vent their rage
When a husband makes a second marriage.   880
But your change of heart is for the better.
It's taken time, but you have recognised
The right decision. That's a sensible woman!
As for you, boys, your father, with due care,
Has made – god willing – your future quite secure.   885
I think that one day you will be,
With your new brothers, leading men here in Corinth.
You must grow up. Your father – and any kindly god –
Will take care of the rest.
I want to see you flourish and come to your prime,   890
Victorious over my enemies.
(to Medea) What's this? Eyes wet with fresh tears?
Pale cheeks? Why do you turn away?
Aren't you pleased with what I say?
MEDEA It's nothing. I was thinking of these children.   895
JASON Don't worry. I will arrange well for them.
MEDEA All right. I will trust what you say.
Woman is the weaker sex, and born to tears.

Helios, the Sun God

The Greeks thought of the sun, the most magnificent of heavenly bodies, as a god. However, because he did not, like Zeus and the other Olympian gods, involve himself in human lives, they did not honour him with temples. They regarded him with awe, and invoked him, often as a witness to oaths (see 724, 730), because he 'sees all and hears all'. A few cults of the Sun God existed, notably in Rhodes, but these were of foreign origin. In Aristophanes' comedy *Peace* the hero says 'we Greeks sacrifice to the Olympian gods, whereas the barbarians sacrifice to the Sun and Moon'.

Medea is proud to be descended from the Sun and proud of his magnificent bequest (922). As we shall see, the Chorus desperately appeal to him to stop Medea's plan (1233), but it is his robe and crown which are instrumental in the Princess' death, and he who sends the chariot in which Medea makes her escape (1300).

924 bridal gifts: Strangely, Medea uses the Greek word which is the equivalent of our 'dowry' – the goods which a bride brings to her husband.

The Chorus, in a production directed by Yujio Ninagawa at the National Theatre, 1987.

JASON Why so much moaning for the boys?

MEDEA I gave them birth. When you prayed for their lives,   900
Pity overwhelmed me, wondering about their future.
What you have come to hear from me
Has been in part said; the rest I'll tell you now.
The king has resolved to banish me from here –
It's best for me, I recognise, not to be   905
In your way or the royal family's. They think
I bear some grudge against the family.
And so I leave for exile.
But the boys – beg Creon to spare them banishment,
So you can bring them up.   910

JASON I don't know if I can persuade him: I will try.

MEDEA Then tell your wife to ask her father
To spare the boys from banishment.

JASON Yes, I think she could do that – if she's a woman.

MEDEA And I will help you in the task.   915
I'll send her gifts, the finest in the world:
A finely woven dress and crown of beaten gold.
The boys will take them. Quickly,
Tell a maid to fetch the adornments.
Not once, but countless ways she will be blest: 920
Winning so fine a man as you to share her bed,
And gaining the adornments which the Sun God,
My father's father, bequeathed to his descendants.
Take these bridal gifts, boys, in your hands.
Carry them and give them to the happy royal bride.   925
It is no contemptible gift she will receive.

932 Don't say that: Jason fails to see just how suspicious it is for Medea to be giving away her divine inheritance to someone who is not even a descendant of the Sun, but Medea is nevertheless anxious that he may thwart her plan. Her succession of short sentences (932–7) perhaps shows her concern.

938 go to the rich palace: Medea seems unable to resist this sarcastic reference to Jason's remarks about the wealth of the palace (928).

939 Kneel: Medea sends the boys to exploit the same ritual entreaty which she has used on Creon and Aegeus.

944: At this point Jason leaves the stage with the boys.

Medea and Jason's second meeting

This second scene between Medea and Jason is very different in tone from the first. It is a 'family' scene, staged by Medea, in which she plays the dutiful wife (as the Nurse said she used to be – see 12–14). There are many clues in the text of this scene to help in its staging.

○ What is important to portray in Medea's manner and actions?
○ What is important to portray in Jason's manner and actions?
○ How might the children be portrayed?

FOURTH CHORAL ODE (4TH *STASIMON*) (945–68)

In the first pair of stanzas the Chorus despair of the boys' future. They see both the boys' and the Princess' deaths as now inevitable.

JASON Foolish woman, why part with these?

Do you think the palace is short of dresses?

Or money, do you think? Keep them! Don't give them away.

If my wife thinks me of any worth,   930

She'll put me before valuables, I am sure.

MEDEA Don't say that. 'Gifts win over even the Gods.'

And, with mortals, gold has more power

Than ten thousand words. Luck's with her,

God's on her side. She is the new mistress.   935

To buy my sons from exile,

I'd pay not only gold, but with my life.

Boys, go to the rich palace,

Kneel before your father's new wife, my new mistress.

And beg her to spare you from banishment,   940

Give her the pretty things: this is most important,

Give these presents into her own hands.

Go quickly. Bring back good news to your mother,

That her wishes are fulfilled.

CHORUS Now we have no more hope that the boys can live,   945

No more hope! They are already walking to their death.

The bride will receive the golden coronet,

Receive, unhappy girl, her doom;

With her own hands place on her fair hair

The adornment of death.   950

Won over by their radiant, heavenly beauty,

She will put on the robe and golden crown,

Dressed as the bride of death.

She will fall into the trap,

Unhappy girl, the death that is her fate.

She can't escape her doom.   955

The Chorus' sympathies

In the second pair of verses, the Chorus address in turn (957) Jason, who must have left the stage, and (963) Medea. Note that they continue to highlight Medea's sexual loss (see 148, 416).

- To what extent do the Chorus women here blame and sympathise with Jason and Medea?
- Do you detect any change in their attitudes?

FIFTH EPISODE (969–1050)

The boys return with the Tutor (969).

Suspense and dramatic irony

The audience knows that the Princess has taken the robe and crown (971). We can now only wait for news of her death. Note how Euripides delays this until line 1087.

First, there is an ironic scene between Medea and the Tutor, who does not understand the significance of his news or Medea's response and tries to cheer her up (973–90). Then Medea says farewell to the boys (991–1050). Finally the Chorus discuss the tribulations of parenthood (1051–86).

975 Aiai: Medea's response to the Tutor's news that her plan has been successful is not the cry of triumph which we hear later at the news of the Messenger (1098).

- How do you explain this?

982–3 The gods ... have brought this about: Whatever her other feelings, Medea believes in the gods' support. Here she even sees them as her associates.

You, wretched man, treacherous suitor of a royal marriage,
          Blindly bring upon your children
          Their destruction, and to your wife
               A hideous death.   960
          Unhappy man, how far you've strayed
               From your hopes.

          I share your grief, poor mother of the boys:
          You will murder your own children
               For your bridal bed,   965
               Which he abandoned,
          Flouting right, and lives – your husband –
               With another in his bed.

TUTOR Mistress, your boys here are spared their banishment,
          And the princess was delighted with the presents.   970
          She took them with her own hands.
          So there's peace there for the boys.
          What's this? Why do you stand there so troubled,
          When all is well?
MEDEA Aiai.   975
TUTOR This doesn't chime with my news.
MEDEA Aiai, aiai.
TUTOR Is there something in my news that I don't understand?
          Am I wrong to think that it is good?
MEDEA Your news is what it is. I don't blame you.   980
TUTOR Why are you downcast and weeping?
MEDEA I can't help it, old man. The gods
          And my own evil schemes have brought this about.

986 I'll bring some others home: Medea's words must puzzle the Tutor. They have a second meaning 'I will take some others down to Hades'. Despite this cryptic remark, she tries to maintain the appearance of normality with the Tutor (990). He now leaves the stage.

Medea alone with the children

Once Medea is alone with her sons her resolution wavers. Analyse the speech carefully.

- What insights does this scene offer into Medea's character?
- What thoughts and feelings make her weaken?
- Which thoughts restore her determination?
○ Suggest ways of staging the scene to bring out Medea's dilemma and agony. How much of what she says do the boys hear? (See note on 1022.)

Some scholars question whether the whole of this speech was written by Euripides, suspecting that the second half, from 1026 to the end, was added at some point by an actor.

- What would be the effect, on the play and our understanding of Medea, if this passage were omitted?

Marriage customs (996–7)

The bride was led to her husband's home by torch light. (See also note on 858.)

998 stubborn pride: The Nurse (95) and Jason (602) have already noted this quality (*authadia*) in Medea. She herself is aware of its dangers (212). (See also Index.)

1008 a different sphere of life: Here is another bitter ambiguity.

1010 smile: Again the playwright describes what the mask of the original production could not show. (See also 1044–5.)

TUTOR Take heart. You will come home one day –

  The boys will see to it.   985

MEDEA I'll bring some others home before that.

TUTOR You are not the only mother parted from her children.

  Mortals must bear misfortune lightly.

MEDEA I will. Now go inside,

  Arrange the children's usual needs.   990

  Children, children, now you have a city,

  A home, where, leaving poor me,

  You will live forever parted from your mother.

  I shall go to another land, an exile,

  Before I can have my joy in you, see you happy,   995

  Before I can honour your brides and adorn

  Your marriage beds and hold aloft the marriage torch.

  O misery! O my stubborn pride!

  All for nothing, boys, I brought you up,

  All for nothing tortured myself with toil and care,   1000

  And bore the cruel pains when you were born.

  Once I placed great hopes in you, that you

  Would care for my old age and yourselves

  Shroud my corpse. That would make me envied.

  Now that sweet thought is no more. Parted from you   1005

  I shall lead a grim and painful life.

  You will no longer see your mother with your dear eyes.

  You will have moved to a different sphere of life.

  Oh, oh! Children, why do you keep your eyes on me?

  Why do you smile at me, your last smile?   1010

  Aiai. What am I to do? Women,

  My courage leaves me, when I see their bright expressions.

  I can't do it. I give up my former plan.

  I'll take my children away from Corinth.

  Why should I try to hurt their father by making them suffer,   1015

  And suffer twice as much myself?

  No, I'll give up my plan.

1022 Go, boys, indoors: If the boys go, they must return in time for line 1038. They must certainly leave at line 1046. Though it is important to keep the children in focus, too much movement would be distracting. Perhaps the boys hesitate on leaving, and wait at the side of the stage.

'Sacrifice'

1023 Those for whom it is not right / To be present: Medea's words resemble the formula by which a priest or priestess warns those to leave who are unclean or in any way unfit to be present at a ritual event. Her use of the word 'sacrifice' to describe her plan is extraordinary: nowhere else does she hint that she sees herself as a priestess (who may be exempt from responsibility and guilt).

- Does she have a vision (from which she recoils) of herself 'sacrificing' the boys?
- Or is she using a macabre metaphor?

1028–31 They will live … leave my children:

- If Medea takes the boys to Athens, how is she leaving them for her enemies? Is there some muddled thinking here?

1030 avenging fiends: These are *alastores*, spirits whose role is to ensure that a killing is avenged or atoned for.

1046: The boys finally leave the stage.

Medea's passion

In line 1026 Medea addresses her *thumos* ('Oh, my heart … !'). The Greek word means the place where feeling is located; it has a sort of independent existence. In Epic poetry the *thumos* speaks or is addressed in inner dialogue. It prompts, or deters a person from, action. For example, in *Odyssey ix* Odysseus thinks of killing Cyclops, 'but a second *thumos* checked me'.

- What feeling or passion(s) is Medea appealing to here?

1049 passion masters my resolve: Here *thumos* is translated as 'passion'. Medea means that her rational self cannot control the irrational, passionate element in her. In another of Euripides' plays, *Hippolytus*, Phaedra explains her sexual desire for her stepson similarly: 'We know what is good, but do not act on our knowledge'. The nature of evil behaviour was a subject of topical interest for Euripides' audience. His contemporary, Socrates, is supposed to have thought that man would not do evil if he knew what was right.

- Is Medea right in her analysis of herself?
- Is she, in effect, saying 'I can't help it' and trying to excuse herself?

Oh, what's the matter with me? Do I want
My enemies to laugh at me? Shall I let them off
Unpunished? No, I must go through with it.   1020
What a coward I am, even to allow such weak thoughts.
Go, boys, indoors.
Those for whom it is not right
To be present at my sacrifice, consider your position:
My hand will not fail.   1025
Oh, my heart, don't do it! Leave them,
You wretch, spare the children!
They will live in Athens with me
And make you happy.
No, by all the avenging fiends of Hell,   1030
I cannot leave my children for my enemies
To abuse. In any case,
It's done now, there's no escape.
The crown is on her head, the royal bride
Is dying in her dress. I know it.   1035
I have the saddest road to travel,
And these I'll send on one yet more sad.
And so I want to speak to them. Give me your hand,
Children, give it me to grasp.
Dearest hand, dearest mouth! What a noble body   1040
And face you have!
My blessings on you – but in another place!
Your blessings here your father has destroyed.
Your kiss so sweet, so soft your skin;
How lovely a child's breath is!   1045
Go, go! I can no longer look at you.
The horror overwhelms me. I understand
The horror of what I propose to do,
But passion masters my resolve
And passion is the cause of all life's greatest horrors.   1050

CHORAL INTERLUDE (1051–86)

The following lyrical section is not a formal choral ode. It develops a theme from the preceding scene, but in a way which seems more reflective and dispassionate than the Chorus' other contributions. The Chorus respond to the imminent crisis by discussing the advantages and disadvantages – largely the disadvantages – of parenthood. They save to the end the worst horror for parents – the death of a child.

- During this Choral Interlude do the Chorus address Medea? (See note on Staging the ode on page 44.)
- Does Medea hear the Chorus?

Note her state of mind when she next speaks (1087, and see 1098).

- Does this help us to decide what she is doing on stage during the Chorus' singing?

Parenthood

Drama was performed in public festivals to huge audiences. The plays were an integral element in the cultural and intellectual life of fifth-century BC Athens. They were based on traditional stories, but their treatment was often 'contemporary'. This reflected the questioning stance of the age and its concerns with moral, social and political issues. Here Medea's situation provokes a debate – challenging conventional values – on the tribulations which parents can suffer.

- Does this passage seem consistent with the way in which the Corinthian women speak and behave elsewhere in the play?
- How is it appropriate to the dramatic situation?
- Should it be presented as a statement of the whole Chorus or a debate among them?

CHORUS   Often I have been involved in subtle talk,
                    Debates more deep
              Than women should explore.
           But women too feel inspiration –
                 It's part of our nature,   1055
                 Our sort of wisdom.
         Not all, but a few women you will find –
              One perhaps among many –
              Not ungifted by the Muses.

I say that those who are quite without experience   1060
           Of children, or never had their own,
         Are more fortunate than those who have.
         Childless people do not know if children
           Are a joy or grief, but being childless
                 They avoid a lot of trouble.   1065
                 But those who have at home
                  Sweet offspring, I see
              The whole time worn out by care:
              First, how best to bring them up
         And bequeath enough for them to live on –   1070
              Though whether their efforts are
           For worthless or for worthy children
                 Is not yet clear.

         But worst of all, there is one misfortune
                 That can afflict all men: 1075
                Suppose they have amassed
                Sufficient wealth, the children
                  Now are in their prime
           And worthy people; then if their fate
                 Should so decree,   1080
         Death speeds away to Hades, bearing off
                Their children's corpses.

SIXTH EPISODE (1087–1225)

Medea and the Messenger
1091 disaster:
- Is this intended to be heard by the Messenger or the Chorus?
- Is this evidence that Medea is in control of herself and enjoying some dissembling?

1101 Are you mad?: The Messenger is a servant. Imagine what it would be like for him, bringing his terrible message, to be faced with Medea's delight (1098–9), eagerness for the details (1105) and effusiveness ('Friend', 1105).

As at line 975, Medea's response to the news is both ironic and highlights her individual viewpoint (556).
- How is this likely to affect the audience's response to her?

The Messenger
In most tragedies a Messenger, usually a slave, reports some important event which has happened indoors or away from the play's setting. His report is often a tour de force, a highly charged 'dramatic' piece of narrative, offering considerable opportunities to the actor.

The origins of such writing lie in the age of oral epic, when professional bards improvised the repertory of heroic tales from which grew the *Iliad* and the *Odyssey*. Similar storytelling techniques to those of the bards can be seen in Messenger speeches: the use of direct speech, colourful metaphor and language and, in particular, vivid detail, which enable the actor to bring his story to life.

How can it be for our good that,
On top of everything, the Gods impose
On mortals this most painful grief,   1085
Just for the sake of having children?

MEDEA Friends, I have long been waiting for the outcome,
Wondering what will happen in the palace.
Look! I see one of Jason's servants coming.
His breathing is agitated, a sign that he   1090
Has news of some fresh disaster.
MESSENGER Medea, you have done a dreadful, wicked thing!
Get away, escape. Take ship or chariot –
Any means – escape!
MEDEA Why should I escape?   1095
MESSENGER She's dead, the princess, and her father, Creon,
Killed by your poison.
MEDEA Wonderful news! You will be counted from now on
Among my friends and benefactors.
MESSENGER What are you saying? Are you in your right mind,   1100
Madam, are you mad? You have wrecked the royal household,
And do you rejoice to hear the news of it?
Does it not frighten you?
MEDEA I can answer you. But take your time,
Friend. Tell me how they died. You'll give me   1105
Double pleasure, if their death was hideous.
MESSENGER When your two boys came with their father
And entered the wedding rooms,
We servants were delighted. We had grieved
At your misfortunes, but now there was much talk   1110
That you and your husband had
Made up your quarrel.

The events in the palace

In the Messenger's speech we are introduced to a character whom we never meet.

- What impression do we get of the Princess, and of her relationship with Jason? (See also 533 and 573.)
- Using the details of the Messenger's speech, dramatise the events in the palace. Or mime the events while one actor says the speech.

It is interesting that, though this scene was not acted on stage, there is a vase painting of it from the fourth century BC (see page 82). This shows how vividly the early actors imprinted the scene on people's imaginations.

Staging this scene

- Do we need to see Medea's reaction to the speech? Or should the Messenger be given the whole focus of attention?

Some kissed the boys' hands, others their fair hair;
I myself was overjoyed and followed with the boys
To the women's quarters.   1115
Our mistress – the one we now defer to, in your place
– Before she saw your pair of boys, had kept her eye
Lovingly on Jason.
But then she pulled her veil over her eyes
And turned away her fair cheek,   1120
Annoyed that they were there. Your husband
Tried to soothe her girlish moodiness and pique:
'Do not,' he said, 'be unfriendly to those I love.
Stop being cross. Turn your head.
Consider you have the same friends as your husband.   1125
Take these gifts and, for my sake, ask your father
To revoke the exile of the boys.'
When she saw the finery, she could not resist
And agreed to all that Jason said. Before your boys
And their father were far from the palace,   1130
She took the embroidered gown and put it on.
She placed the gold crown on her curls,
And, using a bright mirror, she arranged her hair,
Smiling at the lifeless image of herself.
Then she rose from her chair and moved about the room,   1135
Stepping daintily on bare, white feet,
Overjoyed with her present, often twisting back
To see how well the dress fell to her heels.
But what we saw then was frightful.
Her skin changed colour, she staggered sideways,   1140
Limbs shaking, and collapsed into her chair –
Or she would have fallen to the floor.

1144–5 the anger of Pan … ritual cry: Pan is associated with Arcadia and is a god of mountain herdsmen. Like them, he plays the pipe. He is lustful and playful, and often represented as a goat. He was thought sometimes to be the cause of groundless fear ('panic'). Here the old woman attendant, thinking this was the explanation of the Princess' behaviour, let out the sort of cry (*ololygē*) which might have appeased the god.

1160 fire: The crown is the gift of the Sun. (See note on Helios on page 66.)

© Staatliche Antikensammlung und Glyptothek München. Photo: Christa Koppermann.

The central image in this Italian vase painting of c. 330 BC is the death of Creon and his daughter.

And one of her attendants, an old woman, thinking
The anger of Pan or some other God had fallen on her,
Let out a ritual cry. But when she saw   1145
A white froth coming from her mouth,
The pupils of her eyes twisted from their sockets,
The blood drained from her skin, then she let out –
Quite unlike her former cry – a deep-felt wail.
A maid rushed to the king's rooms, another   1150
To her new husband, to tell him what had happened
To his bride. The whole palace resounded
To the clatter of many running feet.
For a time – in which a fast runner might reach
Half-way in a furlong track –   1155
She said nothing, eyes closed.
Then with a frightful scream she woke, poor girl,
Attacked by a double torment.
The gold crown on her head gave off
A monstrous stream of all-consuming fire.   1160
And the fine-spun dress, which the boys had brought,
Was devouring the poor girl's pale flesh.
She jumped up, on fire, and ran
Shaking her head and her long hair this way and that,
Trying to fling off the crown. The gold band   1165
Held tight its grip, and when she shook her head
The fire burnt twice as fiercely.
She fell to the ground, overcome by torment,
Save to her father quite unrecognisable.
Gone was the clear look in her eyes, gone the natural beauty   1170
Of her face. Blood dripped from her head in flaming drops;
Her flesh, torn by the poison's hidden jaws,
Melted from her bones like resin tears.
It was a gruesome sight. We were all
Too scared to touch her body.   1175
Her fate had taught us enough.

1181 **tomb:**
- What does Creon mean by this? Is 'tomb' a metaphor for his old body or is he thinking of his burial? (See Medea 1002–4.)

The Messenger
He does not presume (1197) to comment on Medea's next moves, but his condemnation is clear. He does, however, permit himself a generalised comment (1199–1205), characteristic of a Chorus or lower-order character. (Compare the Nurse, 114–201.)

'Fancy thinkers' (1202)
The Messenger's sequence of thought is 'All human affairs, including success, cleverness and happiness, are insubstantial. Those so-called clever thinkers (the Sophists) who claim to be able to teach us how to be happy are frauds. You may achieve worldly, material success, but real happiness is something else.' (See note on 'Cleverness', page 18.)

The Chorus
The Chorus see the Princess' death as Jason's punishment, which they have always felt deserved; yet they express pity for her.
- Do you find this understandable?

(Some scholars think 1208–10 were added by a sentimental actor; see note on page 72.)

Suddenly her father, poor man, came in. Not knowing
What had happened, he threw himself beside the corpse.
At once he cried out, embraced her, kissed her hands
And said 'Poor child, what God has destroyed   1180
You so undeservedly? Who orphans my aged tomb
Of you? Oh, let me die with you, my child.'
At last he stopped his cries of lamentation;
But when he tried to raise his ancient body,
Then, as ivy clings to laurel stems,   1185
So he stuck to the fine-spun dress.
A dreadful wrestling match began.
He tried to lift his knee, she pulled him down.
When he used force, he tore his old flesh
Off his bones.   1190
At last the ill-fated man gave up the struggle
And breathed out his life,
Overmastered by the horror.
The two bodies lie together, side by side,
Daughter with aged father,   1195
A calamity made for tears.
As for you, Medea, I say nothing.
You yourself will decide how you may avoid
Punishment. Human affairs, I think, not for the first time,
Are mere shadow. I'd say without fear   1200
That those who think that they are clever,
Our fancy thinkers, are likely to commit the greatest folly.
No mortal man is truly happy.
One man as his wealth rolls in can be
More fortunate than another, but happy – no!   1205
CHORUS God has this day, it seems, brought great calamity
On Jason, as he deserved.
Poor daughter of Creon, how we pity
Your fate, now gone to Hades
Because of your marriage to Jason.   1210

1211 I am resolved: The Greek word with which Medea begins this speech (*dedoktai*) is very definite.

1220 where life's misery begins: There is a metaphor in the Greek which refers to the post which marked both the start and end of the 'hairpin' race-track.

1224–5 though you kill them, / You did love them:
- What does this paradox reveal about Medea's concept of love?

How long is Medea on stage?

At line 1225 Medea leaves the stage, where she may have been continuously since her entry at line 203. Whether or not she has left the stage before (see note on 766), she has certainly dominated it.

Plays in Euripides' time were performed usually with no more than three speaking actors. The use of masks made this possible, and perhaps sensible economy had something to do with the convention. In fact *Medea* can be done by just two speaking actors (plus the boys, who speak only off stage, and attendants). Medea dominates each episode – the role could be played by a single actor (which was not so in many plays), making possible a virtuoso performance.

FIFTH CHORAL ODE (5TH *STASIMON*) (1226–71)

This ode can be divided into four sections.

(a) At first the Chorus plunge into a lyrical outburst with a pair of verses (1226–35 and 1236–45). The Greek metre of the verses suggests strong emotion and agitation.

In the first verse they appeal to Earth and the Sun to prevent the murder. The boys are descended from a god, the Sun; only a god or goddess may kill a god's descendant.

Medea's status

Medea's behaviour makes the Chorus think about her birth and status. She is of the Sun's 'golden race' (see note on Helios on page 66), but she has not seemed till now to be more than mortal: for example, at line 381 she fears being killed.

The Chorus call her (1235) a **fiend of vengeance**. A fiend or Fury (*Erinys*) was a supernatural agent whose role was to ensure that a person received his rightful fate (see also 1030). This is a startling phrase. The Chorus have just (1231–2) stressed her mortality; and, as a murderer, she might herself be thought of as a potential *victim* of the avenging Furies. The phrase suggests that the Chorus (and we?) are beginning to see Medea in a new light.

MEDEA Friends, I am resolved as quickly as I can
    To kill the boys and leave this land:
    Not to delay and give them to another's hand
    Less merciful than mine to murder.
    They have to die. And since they must,   1215
    I who gave them birth will kill them.
    Come, arm yourself, my heart. Why do I hesitate
    To act? It is dreadful, but there is no choice.
    Take the sword, my cursed hand, take it,
    Go to where life's misery begins.   1220
    Do not weaken; have no thoughts
    Of children, that you loved them, that they are yours.
    For this one short day forget your children;
    Then mourn: though you kill them,
    You did love them. Mine is a hapless woman's fate.   1225

CHORUS   Earth and radiant beam of the Sun,
           Look down! Look at this lost woman
       Before she lifts her murderous hand to the children,
             Shedding her own blood.
         For they were born of your golden race   1230
        And for the blood of a God to be spilled
           By Man is a fearful thing.
       Heaven-born light, restrain her, stop her,
       Get her out of the house, the murderous
           Accursed fiend of vengeance.   1235

(b) 1236–45: In the second verse the Chorus echo Medea's own sense of the waste of her life (999–1008), and dwell on the disaster which the pollution of blood-guilt will bring on the family.

The shedding of kindred blood

1242–3 Terrible … is the pollution / Of kindred blood: A killer was polluted by the shedding of blood, and the murder of a kinsman was the worst of crimes (see notes on 773 and 820). In early times the family of the victim had a duty to avenge the murder, which led to retributive killings between and within families; the punishment was often visited on the sinner's descendants. This is a frequent theme of tragedy. For example, the fortunes of the House of Pelops, plagued by disaster for generations, provided plots for many plays, including those in which Orestes and his sister Electra fulfilled their duty to avenge the murder of their father, Agamemnon, by their mother Clytemnestra.

The murder

(c) In this next section of lyrics (1246–60) the Chorus' reflections are interrupted by screams from the house. We hear the boys' last pathetic cries for help – made more pathetic by their apparently hearing the Chorus' words (**Yes,** 1254) – and the Chorus' indecision. The boys' entreaty, which the Chorus has already envisaged for us (834–6), does not stop Medea.

The Chorus' lines in this section should probably be shared among several speakers. They wonder if they should intervene, though the doors are in fact barred (1293). In Aeschylus' *Agamemnon*, the Chorus of old men similarly fail to rush indoors to prevent Agamemnon's murder. (See also note on 824.)

1258 stone: This echoes the Nurse's earlier description of Medea (28).

Was it for nothing that you laboured for your sons,
For nothing bore your beloved boys,
Medea, who left behind the blue-grey Clashing Rocks,
Entrance to that least hospitable of seas?
Hapless woman, what is this deadly rage,   1240
That falls upon your heart, this baleful murder?
Terrible for mortals is the pollution
Of kindred blood, spilt on the ground:
There follow sorrows, sent by the gods
Upon a murderous house.   1245

(screams off stage)

Do you hear? Do you hear children crying out?
Oh cursed, ill-fated woman.

BOY 1	What shall I do? How can I escape	
	My mother's hands?	
BOY 2	I don't know, dearest brother. We are lost.	1250
CHORUS	Shall we go in?	
	This is murder.	
	I'm sure we should help the boys.	
BOY 1	Yes, in the name of the gods, help!	
	Help!	1255
BOY 2	The sword snare is closing in.	
CHORUS	Miserable woman, you must be made	
	Of stone or iron, to kill	
	The fruit of your womb,	
	A self-inflicted fate.	1260

One woman only in the past, we hear,
Laid hands on her own beloved sons:
Ino, who was driven mad by the gods,
When Zeus' wife sent her wandering from home.

(d) Ino: In the final section of lyrics (1261–71) the Chorus remove the focus from the present disaster and (as in other plays) try to find a parallel in history or myth. They say they can find only one, Ino.

Ino was the nurse of the god Dionysus. Hera (wife of Zeus), jealous of this young god who was to rival her power, punished those who helped him. She made Ino and her husband Athamas mad. There is more than one version of what followed, but Euripides, looking for a parallel with Medea, makes Ino in her frenzy kill both her sons.

- In what ways are Ino and Medea comparable?
- In what important ways do they differ?
- Does Ino's fate suggest that Medea's fate is similarly sealed?

Staging the lyrical section (1226–71)

This is a dense and highly charged emotional section of the play.

Professor Gilbert Murray wrote 'The Chorus fling themselves on the barred door. They beat in vain against the bars, and the children's voices cry for help from the other side.'

○ How would you stage the scene?

EXODOS (1272–1396)

This was the name given to the final section of a play, at the end of which the Chorus was led off by a flute player. Jason enters at line 1272.

1282 I have come to save …: It is characteristic of Jason's 'blindness' that he thinks the danger to the boys will come from the royal family.

An Italian vase painting (late 4th, early 5th century BC). Medea is in her chariot, the sons mourned below by Jason and the Nurse, with Furies in the corners. Attributed to the Policoro Painter, South Italy.

She, wretched woman, leapt 1265
Into the sea, in the unholy murder
Of her own children: stepping off a cliff
She perished with the two.
What could be more terrible?
Woman's bed, full of suffering, 1270
What troubles you have caused mankind!

JASON You women, standing there by the wall!
Is Medea still in the house, the perpetrator of this outrage,
Or has she fled?
She will either have to hide beneath the earth 1275
Or take wing and fly to the heights of heaven
If she is to escape the punishment of the royal house.
Does she believe that she can kill the country's rulers
And herself escape the palace scot-free?
But it's not her I care about, but the boys. 1280
Those whom she has destroyed will deal with her.
But my boys – I have come to save their lives,
Lest my new relatives do something to avenge
The unholy murder which their mother has committed.
CHORUS Poor man, you do not know what misery you have come to, 1285
Jason, or you would not have spoken so.
JASON What? You mean she intends to kill me too?
CHORUS Your boys are dead. Their mother killed them.
JASON What are you going to tell me? You have destroyed me, woman!
CHORUS The children are no more. You must accept it. 1290

Medea's appearance

1292 Open the door: At a similar point in Aeschylus' *Agamemnon* the central upstage door was opened and the *ekkyklēma*, a round platform often used to depict interior scenes, was wheeled out, with a tableau of Clytemnestra and the dead Agamemnon. The Chorus' words may have led the audience to expect this to happen now, but Euripides creates a spectacularly different ending. Medea appears in a chariot (1300), out of Jason's reach.

We have no help in our manuscripts as to the staging, but Medea must, in the first production, have been either on the roof of the stage building or swung over the stage in the crane (*mēchanē*). In other tragedies the *mēchanē* was reserved for gods, but no use of it can be dated before *Medea*. A vase painting dated about 400 BC shows Medea in a chariot drawn by snakes (see page 90).

● Do Medea's words and behaviour in this scene make her seem more than mortal now?

Jason and Medea

The two meet for their third confrontation.

● In what ways is this a reversal of the first *agōn* (425–608)?

Jason makes light of his own marital infidelity (1317) (for his attitude see lines 548–9). What Medea calls marriage (*gamoi*), Jason refers to as 'bed' or 'sex' (*lekhos*). The difference between Medea's and Jason's view of their marriage vows, which is central to the play, is perhaps summed up in lines 1345–8.

Jason's view of the situation

Jason is so sure of Medea's ultimate doom (1302–3) that he can hardly understand her continuing presence, which pollutes the Sun (1306), even though Medea has told him that the Sun has sent her chariot. Nor can he comprehend a mother killing her children: he is sure that it is because she is a barbarian that Medea could 'bring herself to do it' (1304, 1319). (The Greek verb *etlēs* used here is from the same root as the noun *tolma*, 'fearful nerve' – see note on page 60.)

Jason thinks Medea should pay for the crimes which she committed in Colchis – murder and treason (1311–15) – ignoring that she did them for him.

1312 avenging spirit: This refers to the agent which should have ensured revenge on Medea for her sin, the murder of her brother. (See note on 1030.)

JASON Where did she kill them? Indoors or out here?

CHORUS Open the door, and you will see the murder.

JASON Undo the bolts there, servants! Quickly!

Open up! Let me see the double horror –

The children's bodies and ... take my vengeance on her. 1295

MEDEA Why do you rattle and batter the doors here?

Are you looking for the corpses and me, who did it?

Stop it. If you want me, say what you wish.

You will never lay hands on me again.

This chariot the Sun has given to me, 1300

My father's father, to save me from the hands of enemies.

JASON Hateful creature! O most detestable of women

To the gods and me and all the human race!

You could bring yourself to put to the sword

The children of your womb. You have taken my sons 1305

And destroyed me. And can you still face the Sun

And this Earth, guilty of the most unholy crime?

Curses on you! Now I am sane. But I was mad

To bring you from your home, from your savage land

To a Greek family: a mighty trouble, 1310

Already a traitor to your father and the country

That had nurtured you. The avenging spirit meant for you

The Gods have visited on me: you killed

Your brother at the family hearth and came on board

The Argo, my fair-faced ship. That's how you 1315

Began! You became my bride. You bore my children,

And because of your feelings about our marriage bed,

You killed them. No Greek woman

Could ever have brought herself to do that.

1323 Tyrrhenian Scylla: Among Jason's many insults, branding Medea as inhuman and uncivilised, he likens her to the monstrous Scylla.

Scylla was changed into a monster by the witch Circe. From her cave in a cliff she lowered her six heads to pick off sailors from passing boats. Opposite her was the whirlpool Charybdis, and the two probably represented the difficulty of sailing between the Straits of Messina, between Italy and Sicily (the sea to the west of Italy is the Tyrrhenian). Homer relates Odysseus' passage between them in the *Odyssey xii*.

Medea's speech (1330–9)

- Why might this speech be thought to encapsulate Medea's character and motivation?

Note the formal, rhetorical tone of line 1330.

Yet I rejected them, to marry you, a wife   1320
Who brought me enmity and death,
A lioness, not human,
Wilder than Tyrrhenian Scylla.
No number of reproaches could hurt you, such is your
Audacity. Out of my sight, vile creature,   1325
Child-murderer! I am left to lament my fate.
I shall have no joy of my new-won bride,
And the sons I gave life and nurture to
I shall never speak to alive again. I have lost them.

MEDEA I would have talked at length in reply   1330
To this; but Zeus the Father knows
What I have done for you, and how you've treated me.
I wasn't going to let you show dishonour to my bed
And live a life of pleasure, mocking me –
Nor the princess; nor let Creon marry her to you   1335
And drive me from the country with impunity.
Call me what names you like: a lioness
Or Tyrrhenian Scylla! I've penetrated to your heart
As you deserve!

JASON You suffer too. You share my pain.   1340

MEDEA I do. But being spared your mockery takes away the pain.

JASON My sons! What an evil mother you had!

MEDEA My boys, it was your father's sickness killed you.

JASON But not at least by my hand that they died.

MEDEA No, it was your insult to me, and your new-won marriage.   1345

JASON You really thought this matter of sex made it right to kill them?

MEDEA You think that's a small misfortune for a woman?

JASON Yes, if she's sensible. But to you it is all disaster.

1349 gnaw: Medea is determined to hurt Jason, while he despairs of hurting her (1324 – in both cases the same verb, *daknein*, 'bite', is used). He will suffer more to be left alive – and alone.

1358 Hera Akraia (Hera with the Temple on the Hill): The goddess Hera was Jason's patron in the story of the *Argo*. More importantly, she was associated with the sacred rite of marriage and with childbirth.

Founding a cult

1361 a solemn festival: Often, at the end of his plays, Euripides links his version of a story to a local festival or cult. There were versions of the Medea myth in which the children were killed in the temple of Hera in Corinth and their murder expiated by an annual ceremony. Euripides here provides his own version of the origin of the ceremony which was practised in his own day.

1363 the land of Erechtheus: See note on page 58.

1366–7 relic / Of the *Argo*: Medea, with prophetic power that one usually associates with a god, predicts Jason's death – and a very unheroic one. Jason had dedicated part of the *Argo* as a thank-offering to Hera in her temple. In later life, as he entered the temple, this relic fell on him and killed him. Medea points to the irony that the boat which brought him to his marriage with her will cause his death (see 387–8: his marriage with the Princess also proves 'bitter').

MEDEA The boys are dead. That will gnaw away at you.

JASON No, they live, to avenge their death on you. 1350

MEDEA The Gods know with whom this calamity began.

JASON They know your abominable mind.

MEDEA Go on, hate me! I loathe that bitter tone of yours.

JASON And I hate yours. There is an easy way for us to part.

MEDEA What? What am I to do? I want that too. 1355

JASON Give me my sons' bodies, to bury and to mourn.

MEDEA No! I will bury them with my own hand. I'll take
　　Them to the sanctuary of Hera Akraia,
　　Where none of my enemies may violate them
　　By desecrating their graves. Here in Sisyphus' land 1360
　　I will establish for the future a solemn festival
　　And rites, to expiate this impious killing.
　　I myself shall go to the land of Erechtheus
　　To live with Aegeus, son of Pandion.
　　You will, as is fitting, die ignobly, 1365
　　Struck on the head by a falling relic
　　Of the *Argo*, a bitter ending to your
　　Marrying me.

The final section of the play (1369–1400) is lyrical (Jason and Medea would have sung their words) and the play ends on a note of emotional intensity.

Medea's status

Is she more than mortal? Medea is nowhere said to be a god, but certainly she has some of the qualities of gods in other plays by Euripides. For example, her obsessive, merciless determination to have the respect which is her due reminds us of Aphrodite in *Hippolytus* and Dionysus in the *Bacchae*. Also in setting up a cult as consolation for the dead she resembles Artemis at the end of *Hippolytus*.

The following considerations are relevant.

(a) At the end of the play Medea is almost certainly above the stage. (See note on page 92.)
(b) Her language has a judgmental authority, typical of a Euripidean god.
(c) She has prophetic power: she foretells (1365) Jason's death.
(d) She is carried away, by the help of a god, to settle in Athens. Uniquely in extant plays, she appears to suffer no punishment for a crime which she (1362 and 773), as well as the Chorus (1266) and Jason (1307), knows to be unholy.
(e) She announces the foundation of a cult practised in Corinth in Euripides' day (1361). Usually it was a god, providing a denouement (*deus ex machina*), who did this.

Another argument starts from the fact that, from ancient times, strong passions and irrational impulses – those forces which are beyond our control but influence and govern our behaviour, such as love, hatred and ambition – could be called 'gods' (*theoi*). Especially in the sceptical climate of Euripides' day, there was a tendency to rationalise religion in this way. Thus, Medea, who begins the play as a wronged woman, is seized by rage and desire for revenge and becomes, by the end, the personification of female vengeance, an irresistible force, merciless even to those whom she most loves.

Though Medea is nowhere called a *theos*, the full force of the tragic violence which she unleashes might be said to be expressed in the way in which she appears in the final scene. Whatever her precise status – with qualities of god, Fury, human being and animal (to which Jason draws attention, 1322 and 1390) – Medea has an awesome power in this scene.

JASON	May the boys' Avenging Fury
	And Bloody Justice destroy you! 1370
MEDEA	What God or Spirit listens to you,
	Who break your oaths and cheat your friends?
JASON	Loathsome child-murderer!
MEDEA	Go home and bury your wife!
JASON	I go, bereft of my two boys. 1375
MEDEA	It is too early to mourn.
	Wait till you are old.
JASON	Dearest children.
MEDEA	Dearest to their mother, not to you.
JASON	Yet you murdered them. 1380
MEDEA	Yes, to cause you grief.

The chariot

Aristotle criticised the sort of play ending which relies on an external intervention for which the audience is not prepared, giving *Medea* as his example. In fact there are much more typical examples in Euripides' work of the *deus ex machina* (in which a god appeared in the crane to tie together the plot), for example Castor and Pollux in *Electra*. Sophocles used the device in only one extant play, *Philoctetes*.

- Why did Euripides introduce the chariot?
- What does it add to our view of Medea, to the dramatic significance and to the visual aspect of the final scene?

Sympathies

- What is the balance of sympathy for the characters at the end of the play?
- Can sympathy for Jason's situation be separated from sympathy for his character?

Note the frequency and increasing desperation of Jason's appeals to the gods and avenging spirits, and Medea's taunt about their futility (1371–2).

Medea seems to seal her triumph at 1371–2 but Jason has the last word.

Staging the final scene

Is Jason alone at the end? Jason could enter at 1272 with attendants: these could be the servants whom he tells to open the doors (1293). Otherwise, he will be calling to servants inside to open up.

- Are there advantages to Jason being alone?
- What effects should one aim at in staging the ending?
- Does Medea 'fly' away? If so, when?
- Does Jason leave at the end of his final speech? If not, why?

Epilogue (1397–1401)

These final lines of the Chorus are appended in our manuscripts to several plays by Euripides. 'Here they seem a little inapposite' (Professor Denys Page).

- Do you agree?
- Suggest reasons for keeping the lines.

JASON Oh, I long to kiss my sons' dear mouths,
To hold them tight.

MEDEA Now you want to talk to them, now embrace them.
And, before, you banished them.

JASON For God's sake, let me touch their tender skin.

MEDEA Impossible. You are wasting words.

JASON Zeus, do you hear how I am driven off,
How treated by this loathsome murderer
Of children, this savage lioness?
As long as I have opportunity and strength,
I will lament and call the Gods to witness
That you killed my children and refuse
To let me touch or bury them.
I wish I had never had children and lived
To see them destroyed by you.

CHORUS Many are the destinies that Zeus in Olympus ordains,
Many things the Gods bring to unexpected ends.
What seemed likely does not come to pass
And, for the unlikely, God finds a way.
So ended this story.

Synopsis of the play

PROLOGUE (1–120)

Medea's Nurse announces that Jason has deserted her mistress for the daughter of Creon, king of Corinth. She regrets Jason's voyage to Colchis, where Medea fell in love with him and betrayed her father and country. Medea had then fled with Jason to Iolcus, where she was responsible for the death of King Pelias, and thence to Corinth, where the family has now taken refuge. The Nurse is alarmed by Medea's anger and inconsolable grief. She thinks Medea is dangerous and that she takes no pleasure in her sons.

The Tutor arrives with Medea's sons and reports that he has overheard that Creon intends to banish Medea and the boys from Corinth. The Nurse warns the Tutor to keep the boys away from Medea in her present mood. Medea's voice is heard cursing her sons, Jason and his whole house. She wants to die. She appeals to the gods because Jason has betrayed the oaths he swore to her.

PARODOS (121–202)

The Chorus enter, worried by Medea's cries, and send the Nurse to ask her to come out of her house.

FIRST EPISODE (203–398)

Medea enters. She bewails the lot of women, their insecurity and dependence in marriage. Her own situation, as a foreigner as well as a wronged wife, is even worse. If she can devise revenge on Jason, she asks the Chorus to say nothing.

Creon arrives and banishes Medea because he has heard that Medea is threatening his family. He fears her rejection by Jason will provoke some violent retaliation from her, and he knows that she is clever and skilled in magic. She insists she has no quarrel with him, only with Jason. Despite his distrust, he yields to her entreaty that she be allowed to stay one more day to prepare for exile.

To the sympathetic Chorus, Medea reveals her intention to kill Creon, his daughter and Jason. She swears by Hecate that the new marriage will have a bitter ending.

FIRST CHORAL ODE (399–424)

The Chorus are exultant. They identify totally with Medea's desire for revenge and speak of a new age dawning for women, in which men will no longer be able to present women as the only wrongdoers. They sympathise with Medea's plight and lament the moral crisis in Greece which the faithlessness of men like Jason has created.

SECOND EPISODE (425–608)

Jason arrives to reproach Medea for her threats to the royal family, and offers money to help her in exile. Medea vilifies him, listing all her services to him, condemning his ingratitude and betrayal of his oaths.

Jason says he owes more to Aphrodite than to Medea. He also says that bringing Medea to civilised Greece was a greater service to her than anything she did for him. In marrying the Princess he is still thinking of the welfare of his children and Medea; she should be grateful. He says her sexual jealousy has allowed her to get things out of proportion. It is her own fault that she is banished, and she is foolish to refuse help.

SECOND CHORAL ODE (609–39)

The Chorus pray that they do not suffer from excessive or adulterous passion, or from the fate of stateless, friendless exile.

THIRD EPISODE (640–802)

Aegeus, who is King of Athens, enters. He is en route from Delphi where he has consulted the oracle about his childlessness. Medea offers to help him cure his problem, and in return secures from him a promise of asylum in Athens.

With this security Medea reveals to the Chorus her plans: to pretend to submit to Jason, and to send her sons to plead with Creon that they may be allowed to stay in Corinth. They will take a crown and poisoned robe for the Princess which will kill her when she puts it on. Medea will then kill her sons. In this way she will hurt Jason most and avoid the mockery of her enemies.

THIRD CHORAL ODE (803–36)

The Chorus, appalled by the plan, sing the praises of Athens, a sacred place which Medea as a murderer would pollute. They can only hope that she will not be able to harden her heart to kill her own children.

FOURTH EPISODE (837–944)

Jason enters. Medea plays the submissive wife and professes to accept all Jason's arguments and asks his pardon. Jason agrees to try to persuade the royal family to let the boys stay. She gives the boys the crown and robe with instructions to put them directly into the Princess' hands.

FOURTH CHORAL ODE (945–68)

The Chorus are now bereft of all hope and anticipate the Princess' death. Jason has brought destruction on his sons and his new wife.

FIFTH EPISODE (969–1050)

The Tutor returns with the boys, announcing that the Princess took the presents and that the boys have been allowed to stay. Medea is agitated. Alone with the boys, she is overwhelmed by what she plans to do and, unnerved by their presence, her courage falters. But finally it is her passion for revenge which prevails and she sends them indoors.

CHORAL INTERLUDE (1051–86)

The Chorus discuss the cares and troubles of having children: even for a good parent the worst of fates, that your child may die, is always possible.

SIXTH EPISODE (1087–1225)

A Messenger comes with the news of the catastrophe in the palace: the Princess has been consumed by the poisoned gifts, and her father Creon has also been killed as he tried to save her. Medea steels herself to kill the boys, which she thinks now is unavoidable.

FIFTH CHORAL ODE (1226–71)

The Chorus appeal to Earth and Light to stop the murder. They implore Medea to avoid the pollution and the awful consequences of spilling kindred blood.

The boys' screams are heard. The Chorus can find only one parallel to Medea's crime: that of Ino, who was maddened by the Gods, and threw herself into the sea with her two sons.

EXODOS (1272–1401)

Jason rushes in to save the boys, but is appalled to hear that they are already dead and at Medea's hands. Medea appears above in a chariot sent by the Sun. Jason's anguished insults, calling her inhuman, are powerless. She is sure of the gods' support. She foretells Jason's ignominious death, and tells him that she plans to bury the boys in Hera's sanctuary where she will establish an annual ritual to expiate the killing.

As Medea leaves for Athens, Jason appeals to the gods to witness her guilt.

The final scene, Almeida Theatre production, 1992.

Pronunciation of names

To attempt an authentic pronunciation of Classical Greek names presents great difficulties. It is perhaps easiest to accept the conventional anglicised versions of the familiar names (e.g. Jason, Zeus). The key below offers help with the pronunciation of all the names in the play, which will give a reasonable overall consistency. Note that the stress occurs on the italicized syllable.

KEY

ay – as in 'hay'
ai – as in 'hair'
ō – long 'o', as in 'go'
ch – as in Scottish 'loch'

Aegeus	E-*jay*-us
Apollo	A-*poll*-ō
Artemis	*Ar*-te-mis
Cephisus	Kai-*fiss*-us
Colchis	*Kol*-kis
Creon	*Kre*-ōn
Erechtheus	E-*rech*-thyus
Hades	*Hay*-dees
Hecate	*He*-ka-te
Hellas	*Hel*-las
Hera	*Hai*-ra
Ino	*Ee*-nō
Iolcus	I-*ol*-kus
Jason	*Jay*-son
Medea	Mai-*day*-a
Pallas	*Pal*-las
Pandion	Pan-*dee*-ōn
Peirene	Pai-*rai*-nai
Pelias	*Pe*-li-as
Pelion	*Pai*-li-on
Phoebus	*Phee*-bus
Pieria	Pi-*e*-ri-a
Pontus	*Pon*-tus
Scylla	*Sil*-la
Themis	*The*-mis
Tyrrhenian	Ti-*rai*-ni-an
Zeus	Zyoos

Introduction to the Greek Theatre

Theātron, the Greek word that gave us 'theatre' in English meant both 'viewing place' and the assembled viewers. These ancient viewers (*theātai*) were in some ways very different from their modern counterparts. For a start, they were participants in a religious festival, and they went to watch plays only on certain days in the year, when shows were put on in honour of Dionysus. At Athens, where drama developed many of its most significant traditions, the main Dionysus festival, held in the spring, was one of the most important events in the city's calendar, attracting large numbers of citizens and visitors from elsewhere in the Greek world. It is not known for certain whether women attended; if any did, they were more likely to be visitors than the wives of Athenian citizens.

The festival was also a great sporting occasion. Performances designed to win the god's favour needed spectators to witness and share in the event, just as the athletic contests did at Olympia or Delphi, and one of the ways in which the spectators got involved was through competition. What they saw were three sets of three tragedies plus a satyr play, five separate comedies and as many as twenty song-and-dance performances called dithyrambs, put on in honour of Dionysus by choruses representing the different 'tribes' into which the citizen body was divided. There was a contest for each different event, with the dithyramb choruses divided into men's and boys' competitions, and a panel of judges determined the winners. The judges were appointed to act on behalf of the city; no doubt they took some notice of the way the audience responded on each occasion. Attendance at these events was on a large scale: we should be thinking of football crowds rather than typical theatre audiences in the modern world.

Like football matches, dramatic festivals were open-air occasions, and the performances were put on in daylight rather than with stage lighting in a darkened auditorium. The ideal performance space in these circumstances was a hollow hillside to seat spectators, with a flat area at the bottom (*orchēstra*) in which the chorusmen could spread out for their dancing and singing and which could be closed off by a stage-building (*skēnē*) acting simultaneously as backdrop, changing room and sounding board. Effective acoustics and good sight-lines were achieved by the kind of design represented in Fig. A on page 108, the theatre of Dionysus at Athens. The famous stone theatre at Epidaurus (Fig. B), built about 330 BC, and often taken as typical, has a circular *orchēstra*, but in the fifth century it was normal practice for

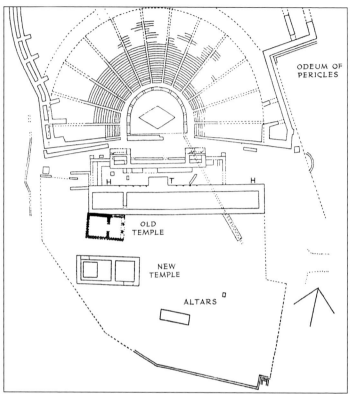

Fig A. *The theatre of Dionysus at Athens.*

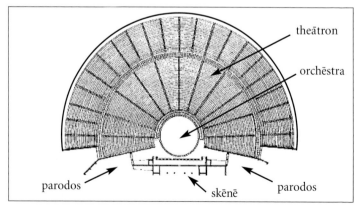

Fig B. *The theatre at Epidaurus (4th century BC).*

theatres to have a low wooden stage in front of the *skēnē*, for use by the actors, who also interacted with the chorus in the *orchēstra*.

Song and dance by choruses and the accompanying music of the piper were integral to all these types of performance and not just to the dithyramb. In tragedy there were 12 (later 15) chorusmen, in comedy 24, and in dithyramb 50; plays were often named after their chorus: Aeschylus' *Persians*, Euripides' *Bacchae*, Aristophanes' *Birds* are familiar examples. The rhythmic movements, groupings and singing of the chorus contributed crucially to the overall impact of each show, ensuring that there was always an animated stage picture even when only one or two actors were in view. The practice of keeping the number of speaking actors normally restricted to three, with doubling of roles by the same actor where necessary, looks odd at first sight, but it makes sense in the special circumstance of Greek theatrical performance. Two factors are particularly relevant: first the use of masks, which was probably felt to be fundamental to shows associated with the cult of Dionysus and which made it easy for an actor to take more than one part within a single play, and second the need to concentrate the audience's attention by keeping the number of possible speakers limited. In a large open acting area some kind of focusing device is important if the spectators are always to be sure where to direct their gaze. The Greek plays that have survived, particuarly the tragedies, are extremely economical in their design, with no sub-plots or complications in the action which audiences might find distracting or confusing. Acting style, too, seems to have relied on large gestures and avoidance of fussy detail; we know from the size of some of the surviving theatres that many spectators would be sitting too far away to catch small-scale gestures or stage business. Some plays make powerful use of props, like Ajax's sword, Philoctetes' bow, or the head of Pentheus in *Bacchae*, but all these are carefully chosen to be easily seen and interpreted.

Above all, actors seem to have depended on their highly trained voices in order to captivate audiences and stir their emotions. By the middle of the fifth century there was a prize for the best actor in the tragic competition, as well as for the playwright and the financial sponsor of the performance (*chorēgos*), and comedy followed suit a little later. What was most admired in the leading actors who were entitled to compete for this prize was the ability to play a series of different and very demanding parts in a single day and to be a brilliant singer as well as a compelling speaker of verse: many of the main parts involve solo songs or complex exchanges between actor and chorus. Overall, the best plays and performances must have offered audiences a great charge of energy and excitement: the chance to see a group of chorusmen dancing and singing in a sequence of different guises, as young maidens, old counsellors, ecstatic maenads, and exuberant satyrs; to watch scenes in which supernatural beings – gods, Furies, ghosts – come into contact with human beings; to listen to intense debates and hear the blood-curdling off-stage cries that heralded the arrival of a messenger with an account of terrifying deeds within, and then to see the bodies brought out and witness the lamentations. Far more 'happened' in most plays than we can easily imagine from the bare text on the page; this must help to account for the continuing appeal of drama throughout antiquity and across the Greco-Roman world.

From the fourth century onwards dramatic festivals became popular wherever there were communities of Greek speakers, and other gods besides Dionysus were honoured with performances of plays. Actors, dancers and musicians organised themselves for professional touring – some of them achieved star status and earned huge fees – and famous old plays were revived as part of the repertoire. Some of the plays that had been first performed for Athenian citizens in the fifth century became classics for very different audiences – women as well as men, Latin speakers as well as Greeks – and took on new kinds of meaning in their new environment. But theatre was very far from being an antiquarian institution: new plays, new dramatic forms like mime and pantomime, changes in theatre design, staging, masks and costumes all demonstrate its continuing vitality in the Hellenistic and Roman periods. Nearly all the Greek plays that have survived into modern times are ones that had a long theatrical life in antiquity; this perhaps helps to explain why modern actors, directors and audiences have been able to rediscover their power.

For further reading: entries in *Oxford Classical Dictionary* (3rd edition) under 'theatre staging, Greek' and 'tragedy, Greek'; J.R. Green, 'The theatre', Ch. 7 of *The Cambridge Ancient History, Plates to Volumes V and VI*, Cambridge, 1994; Richard Green and Eric Handley, *Images of the Greek Theatre*, London, 1995; Rush Rehm, *Greek Tragic Theatre*, London and New York, 1992; P.E. Easterling (ed.), *The Cambridge Companion to Greek Tragedy*, Cambridge, 1997; David Wiles, *Tragedy in Athens*, Cambridge, 1997.

Professor P.E. Easterling

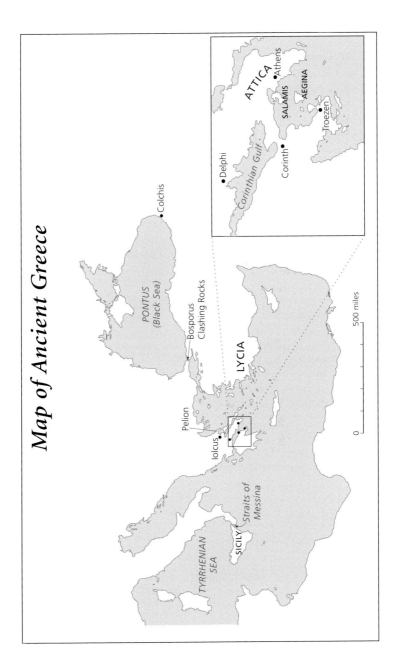

Map of Ancient Greece

PONTUS
(Black Sea)

Colchis

Bosporus
Clashing Rocks

LYCIA

Pelion

Iolcus

Straits of
Messina

TYRRHENIAN
SEA

SICILY

ATTICA

Athens

SALAMIS

AEGINA

Troezen

Delphi

Corinth

Corinthian Gulf

0   500 miles

Time line

Dates of authors and extant works

12th Century BC	The Trojan war	
8th Century BC	**HOMER**	• *The Iliad* • *The Odyssey*
5th Century BC 490–479 431–404	**The Persian wars** **The Peloponnesian wars**	

c. 525/4–456/5
 	
472
467
 	
456
	AESCHYLUS	(In probable order.)
		
		• *Persians*
		• *Seven against Thebes*
		• *Suppliants*
		• Oresteia Trilogy:
		  Agamemnon, Choephoroi
		  Eumenides
		• *Prometheus Bound*

c. 496/5–406 409 401 (posthumous)	**SOPHOCLES**	(Undated plays are in alphabetical order.) • *Ajax* • *Antigone* • *Electra* • *Oedipus* • *Trachiniae* *Tyrannus* • *Philoctetes* • *Oedipus at Colonus*
c. 490/80–407/6 438 (1st production 455) 431 428 415 412 409 ?408 ?408–6	**EURIPIDES**	(In probable order.) • *Alcestis* • *Medea* • *Heracleidae* • *Hippolytus* • *Andromache* • *Hecuba* • *Suppliant Woman* • *Electra* • *Trojan Women* • *Heracles* • *Iphigenia among the Taurians* • *Helen* • *Ion* • *Phoenissae* • *Orestes* • *Cyclops* (satyr-play) • *Bacchae* • *Iphigenia at Aulis*
460/450–c. 386 411 405	**ARISTOPHANES**	 • *Thesmophoriazusae* • *Lysistrata* • *Frogs*
4th Century BC 384–322	**ARISTOTLE**	• *The Art of Poetry*

Index

Numbers refer to lines, unless bold (page).